RUBBER SOLDIERS

The Forgotten Army that Saved the Allies in WWII

DEDICATION

To the thousands of men, recruited from the Brazilian northeast, to tap rubber for the Allied War effort in 1942, known as the "rubber soldiers."

RUBBER SOLDIERS

The Forgotten Army that Saved the Allies in WWII

Gary Neeleman and Rose Neeleman

Schiffer Publishing Ltd

4880 Lower Valley Road • Atglen, PA 19310

Library of Congress Control Number: 2017931602

Cover and interior designed by Matt Goodman
Type set in New Caledonia, Trade Gothic & Bank Gothic.

ISBN: 978-0-7643-5332-1
Printed in China

Published by Schiffer Publishing, Ltd.
4880 Lower Valley Road
Atglen, PA 19310
Phone: (610) 593-1777; Fax: (610) 593-2002
E-mail: Info@schifferbooks.com
Web: www.schifferbooks.com

CONTENTS

ACKNOWLEDGMENTS

The story of the "rubber soldiers" is one of the most dramatic, untold stories of World War II. Outside of Brazil, very few people have ever heard of the saga of the "Rubber Army." In researching this amazing story over the past few years, we have had to rely on the services of several individuals who not only provided us with essential research from the files of the United States (US) Congress, but also the events and rare experiences of thousands of men who worked and gave their lives to assist the Allies in the search for rubber during a critical period of World War II.

Thanks to:

Wade Davis, renowned author, and the lead explorer of the Amazon for National Geographic, for his encouragement, collaboration, and profound knowledge of the history of rubber.

Daniel Goaslind, a bright young intern from the Hinckley Institute at the University of Utah, who, while an intern in the office of Utah Senator Orrin Hatch, spent countless hours digging through US State Department files to uncover original agreements between the governments of American President, Franklin D. Roosevelt, and Brazilian President Getúlio Vargas, which provided the basic understanding between the two countries for the search of rubber in the Amazon basin.

Ariadne Araújo, a journalist and native of the State of Ceará in northeastern Brazil, where most of the rubber soldiers originated. Her insightful reporting of this incredible story provided essential information concerning the migration.

David Neeleman and Mark Neeleman, who worked closely with us in Brazil and helped with the research.

Irlan Rogério Erasmo da Silva, a native of the State of Rondônia, in the city of Porto Velho, heartland of the wild rubber estates in the Amazon. A descendant of the rubber soldiers and attorney for the rubber tappers union who introduced us to the surviving rubber tappers, and provided us with essential information about their lives.

Andrew Moura, a student with dual Brazilian-American citizenship, who worked tirelessly with us in formatting the manuscript, and organizing the exclusive photos in the book.

Mark Grover, a longtime friend and Brazilian expert in the Brigham Young University Latin American section of the library, who served as a consultant and peer as we worked on the book.

PREFACE

From the later part of the nineteenth century, the interests of Brazil and the United States (US) have been intertwined. As a correspondent for United Press International from 1958 to 1966, and having lived in Brazil previously from 1954 to 1957, I became increasingly fascinated by the unusual relationship between the US and the Brazil.

One of my first exposures to the nearly unknown story of this historic commonality was when I stumbled on the story of the Confederate migration to Brazil in 1865. We later chronicled the amazing tale of the heartache and hardships suffered by these Confederate Americans in their new home in Brazil, in a book called, *The Stars and Bars Beneath the Southern Cross: The Confederate Migration to Brazil.* We published this story in Brazil in Portuguese in 2016, *A Migracao Confederado: Estrelas e Barras sob o Cruzeiro do Sul*, by PUCRS University in Porto Alegre, Brazil.

The Confederate story led us to another Brazil-US relationship dating back to 1867 when a northern officer, Col. George Church, was recruited by the Bolivian, and later the Brazilian governments, to build a railroad along the 230-mile stretch of the Madeira-Mamoré River between the cities of Porto Velho and the Bolivian border town, Guajará-Mirim. This railroad was constructed in the heart of the Amazon jungle at a cost of an estimated 10,000 lives, and thirty million dollars. It was built by American engineers, with equipment from Philadelphia, Pennsylvania, and became the main artery of transportation for strategic resources, mainly rubber, for the war effort during the early part of the century, and through World War II. We published the story of this amazing railroad, "*Trilhos na Selva*" (*Tracks in the Jungle*) in 2011 in Portuguese in Brazil, and later in English (*Tracks in the Amazon,* University of Utah Press, 2014).

As we researched *Tracks in the Amazon* in the city of Porto Velho in the Amazon basin, we interviewed several individuals who had relatives who were not only involved in the construction of the Madeira-Mamoré Railroad, but were also descendants of a group of men in that area who, in 1942, were referred to as the "Rubber Soldiers."

One of our main sources on the rubber soldier story was Irlan Rogério Erasmo da Silva, the legal representative of the rubber tappers syndicate. Another was Luís Leite de Oliveira, champion of the movement in Porto Velho to preserve the remnant of the Madeira-Mamoré Railroad and the Madeira River itself. Both of these individuals are natives of the city of Porto Velho, in the Brazilian State of Rondonia, and direct descendants of the original rubber trappers (rubber soldiers).

As we met frequently with these men, and many others in the city of Porto Velho, the incredible story of the Rubber Soldiers unfolded. After dozens of interviews, research in Brazilian publications in the Brazilian northeast in the State of Ceará, and more recent research in the files of the US Department of State in Washington, DC, we have been able to assemble the chronology of an amazing story, which cost an estimated twenty-six thousand lives during the World War II years from 1942 to 1947.

When Pearl Harbor was attacked on 7 December 1941, ninety-seven percent of all of the natural rubber in the world was in the hands of the Japanese. Rubber was an essential ingredient for mounting an effective war machine. From Wade Davis' book, *One River*, everything in World War II depended upon rubber. Sherman tanks have twenty tons of steel and a half-ton of rubber. Five hundred pounds of rubber are in a Dodge truck. There is almost a ton of rubber in a heavy bomber. Each battleship sunk in Pearl Harbor had more than twenty thousand rubber parts. Every ship, every valve and seal, every tire on every truck and plane had rubber. Every inch of wiring in every factory, home and office in America was wrapped in rubber. Conveyor belts, hydraulics, inflatable boats, gas masks, and rain gear are all made of rubber.

During this research, we have come to believe that the thousands of Rubber Soldiers who died in the jungle during those four years from yellow fever, malaria, dengue, beriberi, and dozens of other jungle afflictions may have been the largest sacrifice of any country—other than the US, Great Britain, and France—in the Allied victory in World War II. Brazilian historians say that it was the most deadly war ever fought in Brazil, even though no firearms were used.

These unheralded groups of fifty-five thousand men were solely responsible for the extraction of thousands of tons of desperately needed rubber for the Allied war effort, and they paid the ultimate price without just compensation. Although Brazil lost four hundred fifty-seven soldiers, of the twenty-five thousand who went to Italy as the Brazilian Expeditionary Force (FEB) to fight alongside the Allies, thousands more died in the Amazon jungles in the effort to extract the much needed latex.

CHAPTER 1
THE EARLY HISTORY OF RUBBER

In the foreword of our book, *Tracks in the Amazon*, a history of the Madeira-Mamoré Railroad in the Amazon basin, Dr Wade Davis describes the fascinating history of rubber and its impact on the world. Dr. Davis said:

> The Indians called it *caoutchouc*, the weeping tree, and for generations they had slashed its bark, letting the white milk drip onto leaves, where it could be molded by hand into vessels and sheets, impermeable to the rain.
>
> On his first voyage of discovery, Christopher Columbus encountered Arawakans playing games with strange balls that bounced and flew. Thomas Jefferson and Benjamin Franklin found that small cubes of the stuff were ideal for erasing lead pencil notations, and since they believed the plant hailed from the East Indies, the substance became known as India rubber. In fact, it came from the Amazon, and there, the king of Portugal had already established a flourishing industry that made rubber shoes, capes, and bags. In 1823, a Scot, Charles Macintosh, dissolved rubber in naphtha and made a pliable coating for fabric, which led to the invention of the world's first raincoat.
>
> All of these products, however, had a major flaw. In cold weather, the rubber became so brittle that it cracked like porcelain.

In summer heat, a rubber cape was reduced to a sticky shroud. Then in 1839, quite by accident, an inventor from Boston, Charles Goodyear, dropped a mixture of rubber and sulfur onto a hot stove. It charred like leather, became plastic and elastic. This was the birth of vulcanization, the process that rubber impervious to the elements, transforming it from a curiosity to an essential product of the industrial age. Over the subsequent thirty years, annual production of wild rubber in Brazil soared.

In 1888, John Dunlop invented inflatable rubber tires so that his son could win a tricycle race in Belfast. Seven years later in France, the Michelin Brothers stunned critics by successfully introducing removable pneumatic tires in the Paris-Bordeaux car rally. By 1898, there were more than fifty American automobile companies. Oldsmobile, the first to be commercially successful, sold just four hundred cars in 1901. Less than a decade later the first of fifteen million Model T's rolled off Henry Ford's assembly line. Each vehicle needed rubber, and the only source was the Amazon. In fact, by 1900, Brazil produced ninety-five percent of entire world's rubber.

By 1909, merchants were shipping 500 tons of rubber down river every ten days. A year later, rubber accounted for forty percent of all Brazilian exports. In 1911, production peaked at forty-four thousand two hundred ninety-six tons. It was worth, at a conservative estimate, more than two hundred million dollars.

By 1922, the United States (US) used seventy to eighty percent of all of the rubber production in the world. Although the majority of all of this rubber came from the Amazon basin, as early as the middle of the nineteenth century, Great Britain was frantically trying to break Brazil's corner on the world rubber market.

The flash of wealth was mesmerizing. In Pittsburgh, steel tycoon Andrew Carnegie lamented, "I should have chosen rubber." In London and New York, men and women flipped coins to decide whether to go after gold in the Klondike, or black gold in Brazil. At the height of the rush, five thousand men a week flooded up the Amazon.

Manaus, situated at the heart of the trade in Brazil, grew in a few years from a seedy riverside village into a thriving city where opulence reached bizarre heights. In a city cut-off from the world, flaunting wealth became sport. Rubber barons lit cigars with one hundred dollar bank notes and slaked the thirst of their horses with silver buckets of chilled French champagne. Their wives, disdainful of the muddy waters of the Amazon, sent linens to Portugal to be laundered. In 1907, the citizens of Manaus were the highest per capital consumers of diamonds in the world.

The great symbol of excess, celebrated to this day, was the Manaus Opera House, a monumental Beaux Arts extravaganza designed by a Portuguese architect, and built over a seventeen-year period ending in 1896. The builders, rejecting construction materials of local origin, imported ironwork from Glasgow, marble and gold leaf from Florence, crystal chandeliers from Venice, and sixty-six thousand ceramic tiles from Alsace-Lorraine. Even the massive murals of local jungle scenes were painted in Europe and shipped to Manaus. Operating expenses included subsidies of more than one hundred thousand dollars per performance, the cost of luring established performers across an ocean, and a thousand miles up the Amazon to a lavish venue built in the midst of a malarial swamp.

All of this wealth derived from the latex of three closely related species of wild Hevea that grew scattered across two million square miles of tropical rainforest. In this vast expanse, an area the size of the continental US, there were perhaps three-hundred million individual trees worth exploiting. Finding them was the challenge. In nature, rubber trees grow widely dispersed in the forest, an adaptation that insulates the species from their greatest predator, the South American leaf blight. This disease, found only in the American tropics, invariably proves lethal once trees are concentrated in plantations. It was this accident of biology that forged the fundamental structure of the wild rubber industry.

In order to profit, merchants had to establish exclusive control over enormous territories. Once their lands were secure, they needed workers, thousands of them, in order to gather the latex from the wild. Impoverished peasants were imported from the northeast of Brazil and absorbed into an atrocious system of debt peonage. Then the rubber men turned to the Indians, unleashing a reign of terror unprecedented in the Amazon. As a priest famously wrote of the rubber trade on the Río Putumayo, the river of death, “The best thing that could be said of a white man was that he did not kill his Indians for sport.”

Rubber Soldiers

As the Indians died, rubber production soared. In twelve years that one infamous rubber baron operated on the Putumayo, 4,000 tons of rubber worth seven million five hundred thousand dollars sold on the London market. During that time, the native population on the river fell from over fifty thousand to less than eight thousand. For each ton of rubber produced, ten Indians died and hundreds were left scarred for life.[1]

CHAPTER 2

THE STRUCTURE OF RUBBER GATHERING AND DISTRIBUTION

From the time rubber became an important export product of Brazil in the late nineteenth century, those who produced the rubber, were almost a government unto themselves. Brazil's "rubber elite," who controlled the vast estates of wild rubber trees throughout the Amazon, wielded immense power and were always a problem to Brazil's central government in Rio de Janeiro. The rubber elite wrote their own laws and regulations, and only co-operated with government officials when it benefitted them personally. The rubber elite did not depend on the Brazilian government to defend their interests, transport their products, or regulate their business. The Amazon basin itself was considered a no-man's land, unless one was a part of the rubber elite.

The power of the rubber elite during the time of the empire, when Brazil was under Portuguese rule, was concentrated in the region of Greater Pará, at the mouth of the Amazon River, where the Amazon meets the Atlantic Ocean. Most of the rubber elite were Portuguese, and a few other European nationalities. When Dom Pedro II declared Brazil's independence from Portugal in 1822, the rubber elite of the Amazon were shocked as they seemed to relate much better to Portugal and Europe in general, than to the central Brazilian government in Rio de Janeiro. Under Portuguese domination the rubber elite mostly had their

Rubber Tapper. *Dana Merrill photo, Gary Neeleman Collection*

way with little or no interference from Dom Pedro's empire. The rubber elite had established themselves early in the rubber boom days as the masters of the Amazon, and the possibility of this absolute control being threatened was extremely unsettling to the powerful families that constituted the cartel of the rubber elite. In fact, during the peak period of rubber production, the entire Amazon was almost an isolated economy—selling their rubber and buying commodities and luxury products directly from European suppliers and the rest of Brazil was completely cut out of these transactions, and the rubber elite wanted to keep it that way.

During this period, the rubber elite through their influence in the governments in the various provinces across the Amazon basin, made direct deals with construction companies, suppliers of industrial and manufactured goods, as they worked to improve the infrastructure of the region, including transportation and communications.

The local rubber tappers were obligated to sell all of their rubber production to the rubber elite, known also as *seringalistas*, who in turn sold the rubber to the *aviadores*, or middle men, who would then sell the rubber to foreign companies who had offices in Manaus and Belém. This rubber was then shipped throughout Europe, the United States (US), and other parts of the world.

Up until the rubber was actually delivered to the *aviadores*, very little money ever changed hands. The whole rubber business of the Amazon was on a debit-credit barter system, and the structure was such that the rubber tapper, the low point of the chain, never really got out of debt. Although no one directly controlled the rubber tapper as far as his day-to-day activities were concerned, he was controlled by the fact that he was in perpetual debt. Actually, the rubber tapping season did not cover the entire year, only the dryer summer months, so theoretically the tappers had a window during the winter months when they could do a little farming, hunting and fishing to feed their families and make a little extra money. The rubber tapper himself was responsible for his own territory of between one hundred and two hundred Hevea wild rubber trees, and in order to access these trees, the tapper had to cut trails through the dense forest.

Rubber Tree, Chabloz. *From the archives of the Universidade Federal do Ceará Museum of Art*

The rubber tapper established his own routine which usually consisted of an early morning round to his trees, while it was still relatively cool where he would carefully cut the Hevea tree and place a metal cup near the base of the tree to catch the dripping latex. The cut in the tree was critical as a mistake could kill the tree. The tapper would then return later in the day to gather the latex drippings before returning to his hut to smoke the latex over a smoldering fire through a cone creating a fifty-five-pound latex rubber ball, which would later be sent to a central gathering place.

The tapper usually carried a shotgun to ward off wild animals and threats by Indians. It was a lonely and isolated existence.

Burning the latex. *Dana Merrill photo, Gary Neeleman Collection*

Transporting Rubber Balls to a River Port by Rail. *Dana Merrill photo, Gary Neeleman Collection*

As the demand for rubber increased, there was a chronic shortage of workers to tap the rubber trees and process the latex. As a consequence, the rubber elite began recruiting rubber tappers from the Brazilian northeast. This recruitment process extended through the early years of the rubber boom to about 1913 when the Amazon rubber boom collapsed. Tens of thousands of workers from the State of Ceará returned to their homes as the latex business in the Amazon completely died in the wake of the expansion of the rubber plantations in Southeast Asia.

The relentless quest for the precious latex from wild Hevea brasiliensis tree in the Amazon forest may have not been necessary had Henry Ford, the entrepreneurial industrialist, had his way. From 1927 to 1945, Henry Ford pursued a dream of creating man-made rubber plantations throughout the Amazon, where cultivated rubber trees could be managed and controlled to produce the much sought after latex. The idea that rubber trees could be planted in groves to be harvested systematically, like one would harvest pineapples or avocadoes as it was working in the countries of southeast Asia, could have resolved the problem of the rubber shortage problem facing the US, and Great Britain during World War II. Fordlândia was an amazing and extensive experiment, which failed after many years of effort and investment. Fordlândia was first located about six hundred miles up the Amazon River near the settlement of Santarem where a colony of ex-patriot American Confederate soldiers and their families once settled following the Civil War. Ford negotiated a concession of approximately two million five hundred thousand acres on the banks of the Tapajos River, that was chosen as it was where British botanist, Henry Wickham had collected Hevea seeds in 1876, which resulted in the rubber plantations in Asia. Over a period of years, the Ford team built a replica of an American model city in the heart of the jungle with housing including barracks for a thousand men, three schools, hospitals, sports facilities, churches, and parks. There was a modern sewage and water system, two hundred homes for families, a rail spur, paved roads, and a deep-water port. One school of thought as to the failure of the Fordlândia project was that the very nature of this "American style" community was diametrically opposite to the culture of the region. For example, local workers rejected the cafeteria-style food, the moral restrictions on worker behavior after hours, and the attempt by Ford management, imported from the Detroit, Michigan, to discipline workers.

The Ford project also generated animosity among the rubber elite as they felt the project would have been competition to the traditional business structure of the Amazon. In reality, the main reason for the failure of the project was a fungus, or South American leaf blight, which affected the Hevea trees of the Ford plantation, the seeds of which came from Southeast Asia, and were particularly sensitive to the blight. The Ford executives first noted, "As the upper branches of the young trees began to close in, creating a canopy over the fields … became virulent in the plantations. Within a year it ravaged most of Fordlândia.[1]

Undaunted, Ford instructed his managers to find a different site and try again. In 1934, the Brazilian government agreed to trade seven hundred thousand acres of Fordlândia for a new concession located near the mouth of the Tapajós, just thirty miles south of the city of Santarém. Once again, thousands of acres were cleared, some five million seeds were planted and the infrastructure of a small city was created. This time the scale was even larger. In addition to the hospital, churches, schools, movie theaters, sawmills, machine shops, barracks, roads, power plants, and water works, there were eight hundred houses, three recreational halls, a golf course, and five regulation soccer fields.[2]

By 1941, there were seven thousand people living at Belterra, and three million six hundred thousand trees had been planted. Initially, it appeared that they had found the secret to conquering the blight, but once again, the blight took its toll and the Belterra project also failed. Many of the cultural mistakes which plagued the Fordlândia project were corrected in the Belterra experiment, and worker moral improved but in spite of all of this, continued outbreaks of the blight and cheap rubber from Asia over a thirty year span doomed Ford's efforts to failure. Had Ford succeeded, the US, and Great Britain would have had enough rubber to satisfy their wartime needs, and there would have never been a second cycle of rubber soldiers.

When a military coup installed Getúlio Vargas as authoritarian leader in 1930, Vargas felt his responsibility and destiny was to unite the vast nation of Brazil, and bring the Amazon region, with its many resources, under central government control. He knew early that this was a daunting task, but the world war that erupted in 1941 gave him an opportunity to do things he had never been able to do before.

The Amazon region legally belonged to Brazil, but it was not unlike the wild western part of the US in the 1800s. It was characterized by lawlessness with little control from Brazil's central or even regional government. There were confrontations between settlers in the region and the indigenous tribes, who resented the encroachment of European fortune seekers. The economy was based on a boom and bust situation, depending upon Amazonian products that might be in demand outside of Brazil.

In October 1940, Vargas became the first Brazilian president ever to visit the Amazon. In a speech in Manaus, Vargas outlined the policy of the *Estado Novo* toward the region. Vargas declared that over the past centuries, Brazil's task had been, "to conquer the land, dominate the waters, and subject the forests." Having conquered the "river sea," the next objective was to increase its population in an environment that had been considered inhospitable to civilization. Vargas claimed that new technologies had made it possible to plant a unique civilization that could prosper on the margins of the rivers in the Amazon basin.[3]

Vargas continued as the leader until 1945, and was then elected President of Brazil in 1951–1954, which gave him the opportunity to continue with his early plans to unite Brazil under one central government. Among other things, he made Portuguese Brazil's official language.

Authoritarian and nationalist, Vargas sought to transform Brazil into a modern nation-state by centralizing government, promoting industrialization, and integrating frontier regions into the Brazilian nation. In contrast to the *laissez-faire* economic policies of Old Republic governments, Vargas implemented policies of state-led industrialization, encouraged import-substitution industries, and imposed the government as the arbiter of labor-management relations. An economic nationalist, Vargas sought to diversify and strengthen Brazil's economy through industrialization and insert the state into the management and allocation of the nation's natural resources.[4]

Studies written on the "Battle for Rubber" by Pedro Martinello, Lúcia Arrais Morales, and María Verónica Secreto focus primarily on the impact of the federal government's measures to colonize and develop the Amazon on the rural poor—including rubber tappers, indigenous groups and other Amazonian workers. Rather than blame Amazonian rubber elites for a second cycle of abuse and exploitation of migrant rubber tappers, and native Amazonian rural workers (*caboclos*) during World War II, these scholars criticize the Vargas government for adopting a pro-labor discourse during the recruitment phase and then abandoning the rubber soldiers to their fates after they arrived at the rubber estates. Given the dismal conditions of the rural poor in Brazil, Vargas' pro-labor discourse provoked justified charges of hypocrisy, and hidden political agendas.

Vargas, like many authoritarian leaders, was a master communicator and his most useful tool was radio. The fact that many of the rural poor and uneducated could not read gave Vargas an opportunity to incorporate them through radio into his vast army supporters. Vargas installed a special Department of Press and Propaganda (DIP) to make absolutely certain that the people of Brazil only received positive press reports about him and his regime. In fact, in his effort to control the press, he provided special considerations to the working press such as no income tax, and free access to not only state sponsored events, but also entertainment venues by simply showing a press credential. While living in Brazil as a foreign correspondent, even those of us representing American and European media, received the same considerations long after Vargas was gone. It took years to reverse many of the things that Vargas did to influence not only the media, but also labor laws.

Although Vargas' program to recruit rubber soldiers to extract rubber in the Amazon was ostensibly a campaign to support the wartime alliance, Lúcia Arrais Morales suggests that his real objective was to advance the government's long-term goal of moving marginal populations of rural poor from the northeast to occupy the Amazonian frontier. Morales's anthropological study of the rubber soldiers places the World War II migration in the context of historic and recurring migration patterns between the northeast and the Amazon.[5]

Whereas, before the advent of World War II, the rubber elite in the Amazon controlled almost all of the rubber business in the region, the Vargas influence precipitated significant changes in the culture. For the first time, government became a factor in the gathering and distribution of rubber. The accords between the Vargas government and the government of the US, for example, established price controls on raw rubber, and the rubber elite were not always in agreement with these changes.[6]

After the collapse of the rubber boom in 1912, many international shipping lines departed from the Amazon. During the 1920s and 1930s, subsidies from the Brazilian federal government, as well as the states of Amazonas and Pará, enabled private steamship companies to continue to transport passengers, supplies and raw materials in the Amazon. In 1940, the federal government intervened to end the subsidies and created a government-owned shipping company, Amazon Navigational and Administrational Service of the Port of Pará (SNAPP, Serviço de Navegação e Administração dos Portos do Pará). SNAPP had fifty-two floating vessels, including ocean-going ships, riverboats, tugboats, and motor boats in its 1940 inventory.[7]

Much of the fleet was antiquated, with vessels still burning wood for fuel. The US Rubber Development Corporation (RDC) collaborated with SNAPP to transport the workers and supplies to the rubber estates. The RDC helped to modernize SNAPP by supplying up-to-date ships and riverboats, as well as expert mechanics, welders, and electricians to train Brazilian technicians, and delivering coal and other fuel to Belém at fixed, subsidized prices.[8]

In an agreement with the RDC, concluded in July 1943, SNAPP committed to: maintain the fleet of vessels supplied by the RDC; give priority to any RDC cargo or cargo that was necessary to the rubber program; construct or charter riverboats that could navigate the upper Amazon, where deep draught ships could not go, due to waterfalls and rapids, as well as seasonal changes in river depths; and abstain from making profits from operating boats provided by the RDC and return vessels supplied by the RDC upon expiration of the agreement.[9]

Both the Vargas and US governments attempted to change the old business culture of the region, but found it nearly impossible to buck the system. The rubber elite resented government interference in the management of their rubber estates, and the management and distribution of supplies and food to the workers with price controls and government oversight. Government agencies for the first time established rubber quotas, and in order to provide lower prices for goods and foodstuffs to the rubber tappers, government agencies facilitated the delivery of goods, from the US and southern Brazil.

Obviously, this new structure meant that traditional businesses involved in the collecting and distribution of rubber would either have lost profitability or were forced out of business completely. Eventually, with mounting pressure and a lack of cooperation from rubber elite, the US and Vargas government determined that the new system could not work.

CHAPTER 3
THE STRUGGLE FOR RUBBER

The Brazilians have always said and believed that God is a Brazilian, and the angels speak Portuguese. They go even further when they say, "What man destroys in Brazil by day, God builds back by night." If one takes a few minutes to consider Brazil's vast natural wealth, one could almost agree with the Brazilian theory.

It was already well-known that rubber could be derived from as many as one hundred different species of plants. For sixty years, the British had depended on Ficus elastica, a native of Asia that flourished along the floodplain of the Brahmaputra River. Ruthless exploitation of the wild plantations, and failure to successfully establish the tree in plantations forced them to seek alternatives. In the Congo, the Belgians were harvesting the thick latex of Landolphia, a forest liana. The natives of Mexico and the West Indies extracted good rubber from Castilla elastica, a wild tree in the fig family. By far, the best rubber on the market and the most expensive was called Pará Hard Fine—derived from a species of Hevea.[1]

Without question, the Hevea brasiliensis tree, found only deep in the Amazon jungle, had to have been one of God's greatest gifts to mankind as a source of the finest latex in the world. These incredible trees, and their product, were coveted by all of the industrialized nations on earth. The frantic and relentless quest for the seeds of these amazing trees began as far back as 1880, when the unique qualities of natural rubber were first discovered.

Chapter 3: The Struggle for Rubber

Henry Wickham

As the industrial revolution began to sweep the world, the great powers not only became resentful of Brazil's lock on all of the world's rubber, they also began a determined effort to somehow break the Brazilian cartel. Countless men made an effort to smuggle the precious rubber seeds out of Brazil; but all failed. The seeds would ferment or sprout prematurely at sea. But, there was one man who had a different philosophy than the Brazilians concerning ownership of the precious latex. His name was Henry Wickham.

Wickham, born 29 May 1846, in London, England, was an amateur botanist, adventurer, and a vagabond of the jungle. In spite of this image among his fellow countrymen, Wickham was fiercely loyal to the British Empire, and he made an early decision to chase down the precious seeds and find a way to get them back to England.

Wickham's philosophy was that the world's resources actually belonged to mankind, not individual nations. He felt that the British Empire had a God-given responsibility to be the custodian of the world's resources, and that he should be an instrument to deliver the amazing latex to England where they would be responsible for its development and worldwide distribution. In Wickham's day, bio-piracy was not uncommon, and he was inspired by countryman, Clements R. Markham, who had stolen the seeds of the Cinchona tree, also in the Amazon, which was the source of quinine, the only remedy for jungle fever at that time.

On 23 May 1860, Markham put the seeds of the Cinchona tree on a steam ship to England. Many of the plants died, but eventually enough of these incredible seeds survived and were ultimately planted in Northern India in 1861, and Markham became one of England's heroes. By 1870, the precious quinine produced in the British colonies was saving lives throughout the entire tropical world.

Markham was not the only biopirate of his time, and there were many other examples of biopiracy, that took place. A good example was the Hawaiian pineapple, which came from Central America; tobacco was also an example, which was successfully transferred from one country to another. Probably one of the most famous biotransfers was Brazilian coffee, which originally came from Arabia in 1847. So, Brazil was not only a victim of biopiracy, but also a country, which profited from biopiracy, as coffee later replaced rubber as Brazil's most important export.

When Henry Wickham decided that it was his divine responsibility to deliver latex to the British Empire, he went about his mission with intense focus.[2] In July 1874, Hooker and Markham agreed to pay Wickham ten pounds for every thousand rubber seeds he managed to ship out of the Amazon. Like so many before him, Wickham had countless failures as he tried to gather rubber seeds from the Hevea brasiliensis tree—found only in the Brazilian Amazon. He not only gathered many of the seeds, but he also paid collectors throughout the jungle to gather seeds for him. And, although only an amateur botanist, his understanding of the Hevea brasiliensis seeds increased over time, and he began to experiment with methods of preserving these unusual seeds for eventual transport to England. Finally, by 1876, Wickham had in his possession an estimated seventy thousand Hevea brasiliensis seeds, but was still trying to find a way to transport them to London.

Through all of Wickham's trials and tribulations, his faithful and long-suffering wife, Violate Carter, accompanied him. In fact, he also brought to Santarem, five hundred miles from Belém on the lower Amazon, his sister (Harriett), his mother, and the mother-in-law to his brother (John).

In that year, because of a quirk of fate, one of the newly built stern wheel steamers, the *Amazonas*, sailed up the Amazon on a cargo run. The crew abandoned ship while docked in Santarém and stole most of the cargo, leaving the young captain distraught. When Wickham discovered this, he saw his opportunity and convinced the captain to accept his load of the 70,000 seeds. The fact that the stern-wheeler was considerably faster than the early sailing ships, reasoned Wickham, it could carry the seeds to England without fermentation and premature sprouting. His many months of working with the seeds enabled him to pack the seeds in the hold of the Amazonas to not only keep them dry, but also to protect them from undue exposure. But, when he left on the *Amazonas* for England, he left behind his other family members who later all died of jungle illnesses in Santarém.

While all of this was taking place, the director, Joseph Dalton Hooker, of the Royal Botanical Gardens in Kew, London, had started to doubt the ability of Wickham to succeed in the project, and they had already assigned another of their more scholarly botanists to do the job. It was not until the end of his life that his government finally realized Wickham's genius in gathering, processing and packing these unusual seeds, and finally succeeding in transporting them back to England.

Brazilian authorities, although they were beginning to be sensitive to the problem of bio-piracy of some of their precious and exotic plants, were far less vigilant at that time than they should have been. Markham's successful theft of the seeds of the Cinchona tree had raised the consciousness of the Brazilian authorities concerning the risks of biopiracy, but there were few regulations and laws in place by the time Wickham smuggled the seeds.

In anticipation of possible custom problems in the Port of Belém, as the *Amazonas* entered the Atlantic Ocean, Wickham nailed shut the hatches of the hold of the ship and hoped for the best. His luck held when the British honorary consul, who facilitated quick liberation of the ship with authorization to sail, accompanied the customs inspector.

Wickham arrived in Liverpool, England, with his wife (Violate), to a royal welcome and a royal train to Kew Gardens, where the precious seeds were quickly planted and nurtured. It is estimated that only about twenty thousand of the seventy thousand seeds in the shipment survived and germinated, but this was enough to change the course of history. The British sent the young maturing plants to their far-flung colonies throughout Southeast Asia and India, and a new economic order was born.

The Brazilians took some time to realize the incredible wealth of the Amazon basin, and finally banned the exportation of rubber seeds, and other exotic plant species. By then, many of the plants that had been pirated from this unique area of Brazil were already flourishing throughout the world. In 1900, Brazil produced ninety-five percent of the world's rubber, but by 1913, as the Southeast Asian rubber trees began to mature, all of this changed, and by 1922, Brazil was producing only six percent of the world's rubber. Asian rubber, from Wickham's seeds, was much easier and much less expensive to harvest, only a fraction of what it cost to harvest latex from the wild rubbers trees in Brazil (the entire rubber of the far east would eventually be built on the progeny of these original Wickham seeds).[3]

The Brazilian economy was shattered as the industrial powers shifted their purchase of critical rubber to southeast Asia. Brazil called Henry Wickham the "executioner of Amazonas," and the "prince of thieves,"

Wickham by a Rubber Tree.

while England hailed him as the "father of the rubber industry."

It was in Sumatra, and the Dutch colonies beyond the Java Sea where experiments took place that guaranteed the final demise of the Brazilian rubber industry. Working again with material derived from the original Wickham stock, a Dutch botanist named Peter Cramer revealed for the first time the remarkable variability that characterizes the principal species, Hevea brasiliensis. In plantations grown from seed, there was no way to predict latex production in individual trees. The key, Cramer determined, was to select high-yielding clones and propagate them vegetatively. Instead of dispensing seeds, the Dutch patented a method of marketing bud wood from the very best trees. The results were astonishing. An acre of Hevea planted from seeds produced three hundred and fifty pounds of rubber a year. Yields from the first selected clones doubled that figure, and with each successive generation, production doubled once again. In less than a century, some plantations would experience a sevenfold increase in yield, with the best sites ultimately producing as much as three thousand pounds of rubber per acre.[4]

As the rubber industry throughout the British Empire continued to produce billions of dollars from Henry's seeds, Henry claimed he never shared in this good fortune. In Joe Jackson's interesting book, *Thief at the End of the World*, Jackson describes Wickham's final years:

> After that, he was poor, frightfully poor, spending most of his time at the Royal Colonial Club, surrounded by felling imperialists, each spinning their separate tales. Somehow the annual payment of three hundred pounds from the conflicts dried up. On 3 June 1920 (he was sixty-eight years old), he was made Knight's Bachelor on the King's fifty-fifth birthday "for services in connection with

the rubber plantation industry in the Far East," according to a brief notice tucked far back in the (*London*) *Times*.

As Wickham grew older, and after receiving a knighthood, he became even more aggressive in telling his wild tales. This aggravated, even more, those around him and few took his claims seriously.

Four months after his eighty-second birthday, 24 September 1928, he suddenly fell ill. His condition deteriorated, and he passed away quietly three days later, on 27 September, of "senile decay." He'd always believed he was descended from William of Wykeham, the medieval bishop of Winchester, and asked to be buried at the Hampshire village of Wickham. Although the belief was probably mistaken, his wish was fulfilled.

Violet fells ill within a month of him. We know they loved each other. There are secrets we'll never know, but she stood by him through the worst, and he'd loved her so recklessly that he swam a shark-filled channel in the middle of the night just to be with her. He was often a fool, but he was her fool, and for all his faults, he remained brashly, outrageously charming. She was in London and heard of his sickness. There is some suggestion that Henry knew she was in town. But both were too weak to make the trip and reunite. They'd parted over Henry's insatiable attempts for a second success, and Violet's unending loneliness in the world's worst places. They'd loved each other deeply, but rubber and the madness and greed it spawned finally came between them. Both died alone.

On the day after his death, Henry's obituary ran inside the (*London*) *Times*: "Sir Henry Alexander Wickham … was the man who, in the face of extraordinary difficulties, succeeded in smuggling seeds of the Hevea tree from the upper Amazon, and so laid the foundation of the vast plantation rubber industry. Looking every inch a pioneer, broad shouldered and heavily built, with an extraordinarily long and wavy moustache, his physical strength was as great as his resolution. To these qualities he owed his escape from the many adventures, which he encountered in his wanderings. In conversation, he was most entertaining, and his stories were not only interesting but also instructive."[5]

CHAPTER 4

WINDS OF WAR

The British success in pirating the rubber seeds and the Cinchona seeds from Brazil in 1876, is only one example of what other European nations had in mind as far as Latin America was concerned. Most of the major European powers had already had a taste of the seemingly endless wealth of the Latin American region, and each of these European powers felt they needed to have some claim to the riches of the area. Both the Portuguese and Dutch settled vast regions of Brazil, and the Spanish and the French also felt they were entitled to some of this vast wealth. Over the last century, the Germans had a fascination for the South American countries and established large immigrant colonies in the areas of Southern Brazil, Argentina and Bolivia.

It became obvious to the United States (US) that there was a risk that some of these European powers would move into the region—considered to be the backyard of the US—and ultimately dominate the countries of Latin America who were just beginning to assert their individual sovereignty.

In 1823, when the US itself was only forty-seven years old, President James Monroe launched what he called the "Monroe Doctrine." The Monroe Doctrine was designed to isolate Latin America and the Caribbean Islands from any kind of intervention by foreign powers outside of the region.

Early Latin American revolutionaries such as Simon Bolivar and Francisco de Paula Santander embraced the doctrine as being evidence that their countries were recognized, and validated by the United States of America (USA).

In 1861, Spain, France, and England went into Mexico, but with pressure from the US, Spain and England finally withdrew. France stayed until American president Andrew Johnson, following the Civil War in 1865, sent in 50,000 troops to secure Mexico from French domination.

In 1902, Theodore Roosevelt moved the Doctrine in another direction when he determined that the US could intervene in countries that were being poorly administered and Roosevelt's policies prevailed until Franklin Delano Roosevelt launched what he called the "Good Neighbor Policy." The Monroe Doctrine, from the very beginning, was quite controversial and much of the blame for the failures of Latin American governments over the last 150 years has been blamed on the US, for one reason or another. The dictators, military coups, and the rise and fall of Latin American economies have continuously been blamed on the US.

Although there have been many instances in the past half century or more US intervention in one country or another, the possibility of this type of intervention has become less and less. Still, those that know the region well, seem to agree that the tenants of the Monroe Doctrine, where the US must continue to play an important role in the development and preservation of Latin America's young democracies, is still essential and will be for the foreseeable future.

Shortly after World War I, when German nationalism was on the rise, Latin America once again appeared on Germany's radar. With most of the world's rubber being produced in the British colonies in Southeast Asia, from seeds from the Amazon jungle, millions of tons of other strategic materiel was being transported from Brazil, and other Latin American countries, by merchant ships of the British Royal Navy. The new nationalist German government was aware of this and began to lay their plans for control of the south Atlantic.

From the very beginning, merchant shipping to the British was the life-blood of the empire in both peace and war. Although war was still not on the immediate horizon, Germany began to quietly build what was referred to as "pocket battleships," or merchant raiders. The Versailles Treaty restricted these ships to just 10,000 tons, but German ingenuity was able to compensate in size with other technical advantages. In the first place, they had much larger guns, which could fire a shell for over eighteen miles. The ships were built with heavy armor plating, and powerful diesel engines that made them more maneuverable, and more lethal than most any in the Allied fleet. Construction of three of these pocket battleships began as early as 1928, and they were called *Panzerschiff*.

Admiral Graf Spee at Sea.[1]

The first of the *Panzerschiffs* was launched on 7 May 1931. The second *Panzerschiff* was launched just two years later, and the *Admiral Graf Spee*, possibly the most lethal of the three sister ships, was launched 6 January 1936. Besides her heavy guns, the *Admiral Graf Spee* could also fire five torpedoes, and was equipped with many other smaller weapons.

The stated mission of the "*Panzerschiff* raiders" was to destroy and completely annihilate Allied merchant ships. Not only were they to interdict Allied merchant ships carrying strategic materials to Great Britain, the US, and France, but by doing so they were to also lay claim to the vast resources in the South American region.

Just months after World War II erupted in 1939, with the invasion of Poland by Germany, the *Admiral Graf Spee* was already heavily engaged in the "Battle of the Atlantic." The Battle of the Atlantic was described as "a war of tonnage." Early in the war, the *Admiral Graf Spee* sank nine British ships, totaling over 50,000 tons of cargo. It was said that the *Admiral Graf Spee* was a "stain on the Royal Navy."

On 1 May 1940, Germany invaded France, and US, not yet engaged in the war, was being threatened by the Japanese in the Pacific. President Franklin D. Roosevelt was informed that the US had less than a three-month supply of rubber. At this point, the President setup the Rubber Reserve Company to explore ways to increase the US' rubber supply. According to Wade Davis, in his book, *One River*, congress authorized the spending of one hundred forty million dollars to increase the rubber supply, and with the help of the big rubber companies such as Goodyear, Firestone, Goodrich and US Rubber, within months they were able to purchase three hundred thirty-three thousand tons of rubber on the international market, and this bought the US a little more time.

Germany's surface war ships, the *Admiral Graf Spee* and others, were assisted in their battle of the Atlantic by U-boats that patrolled the south Atlantic from the mouth of the Amazon to Argentina, and in the course of the conflict from 1939 to the end of the war in 1945, the Allies lost three thousand five hundred merchant ships, and one hundred seventy-five war ships. Germany lost seven hundred eighty-three U-boats during the conflict.

The US did not enter the war until after the attack on Pearl Harbor on 7 December 1941, so British Naval forces were alone in the south Atlantic during the early stages of the war, and knew they were fighting for survival.

The commander of the *Admiral Graf Spee* was Capt. Hans Langsdorff, a decorated U-boat commander. The dramatic story of how three British light cruisers, the *Exeter*, *Ajax*, and *Achilles* engaged the *Admiral Graf Spee* in the first naval battle of World War II, and ultimately the only naval battle to take place during the war in South America.

Although the *Admiral Graf Spee* was an amazing ship, she had her drawbacks. She was actually too heavy and despite her great firepower, this was ultimately her downfall. As the British warships closed in on the *Admiral Graf Spee*, the *Achilles* suffered serious damage and was sunk. The *Ajax* and *Exeter* continued to shadow the *Admiral Graf Spee*, which was also damaged, as it sailed south toward Argentina. Knowing he was out-numbered, Capt. Langsdorff steered his damaged ship into the Port of Montevideo, Uruguay, where he had hoped to find refuge and an opportunity to repair his damaged ship. Uruguay was a neutral country and was not sympathetic to the German captain, and gave him seventy-two hours to leave port. The German captain flying the swastika spent hours exchanging messages with Uruguayan officials and his superiors in Berlin. Langsdorff decided he had one of two choices: make a run for it and face the British cruisers at the mouth of the harbor, or scuttle his ship. The British had given Langsdorff the impression that reinforcements from the Royal Navy had arrived from the open ocean, and that if he made a run for it, his ship would either be sunk or captured by the Royal Navy; this was unacceptable to Berlin. Consequently, at 1830 on

Sunken *Admiral Graf Spee.*[2]

the night of 17 December 1939, Langsdorff sent the majority of his crew in tugboats up the River Platt toward Argentina and then with his immediate officers abandoned the ship itself as it erupted into a fiery ball. Later, Langsdorff committed suicide in Buenos Aires for having failed his mission.

Today, remnants of the *Admiral Graf Spee* can still be seen in the shallow waters at the mouth of the River Platt, a short distance from the beautiful beaches of Punta del Este, Uruguay.

At this point in the war, after seesawing between Germany and the US to extract the maximum economic benefits from each country, Brazil's ruler, President Getúlio Vargas, became convinced by 1941 that the Allies would win the war.[3]

According to Frank McCann, in his publication, *The Brazilian-American Alliance: 1937–1945*: "Brazil's interests in negotiating an alliance with the US were threefold: to obtain US financing for Brazil's nascent steel industry and other industrial development projects; to bolster the defense of Brazil's coasts from attacks from German submarines and protect its southern flanks from potential attacks by Argentina; and to gain a leadership role in post-war international organizations, including a coveted permanent seat on the United Nationals Security Council" (the latter, obtaining a permanent seat on the United Nations Security Council, has not happened to this day). Surely, this also included the need for the US to finance and guarantee rubber prices, which the US was more than willing to do.

It was only a short time later, that the US entered World War II and joined the British in patrolling and defending the south Atlantic, and the vast merchant ship convoys that carried strategic materials, primarily rubber from the Amazon jungle to the US and Allied ports for the building of the Allied war machine.

CHAPTER 5

UNITED STATES AND BRAZIL ENTER WORLD WAR II

In 1939, at the outset of the war in Europe, Maj. Delos C. Emmons, commander of the United States (US) Army Air Forces, overflew the coast of northeastern Brazil, and concluded that the city of Natal was the most strategic point, both for a possible German invasion of South America, and for the Allies to use as a supporting site for the operations in North Africa. Emmons said Natal would be the Allies' key to defending South America and impeding German expansion in the area. Emmons' assessment of the strategic position of Natal gave impetus to the rapid development, not only of the city of Natal itself, but of the entire area.

Before the war, Natal was a sleepy coastal Brazilian town with only about 40,000 inhabitants. During the war years the city doubled its population to around eighty thousand inhabitants, and experienced vast improvements in its infrastructure.

In that year of 1939, the US was not yet at war with Germany, but they felt it was necessary to begin to fortify, in a subtle way, Brazil's northeastern coast. In an arrangement with Pan American Airways, which was a cosigner, they started a program to develop airfields in the area. The main airfield was Parnamarim in Natal, which during the war became the busiest airfield in the world, with both British and American aircraft landing and taking off every three minutes around the clock. Only an

Natal as a Seaport in the 1940s. *Courtesy of Fairwing Brazil: Tales of the South Atlantic, by John R. Harrison*

eight hour flight to Dakar, the Natal airbase became known as the "spring board to victory," and the most important supply route for troops, aircraft and equipment to reach the battlefronts in Britain and North Africa.[1]

President Vargas certainly wanted to obtain as much modern military equipment and training as possible for his armed forces, in return for Brazil's wartime alliance with the US. But Vargas was also aware that after the leading role, it had played as chairman of the Rio Conference of January 1942, Brazil also needed the protection of the US, not only from increasing numbers of German U-boat attacks on Brazil's shipping, but also from perceived threats to the security of Brazil's southern border from its traditional rival, Argentina, which remained officially neutral but sympathetic to Germany. On 16 February 1942, German U-boats sank their first Brazilian ship, the *Buarque*, soon after it left the port of Belém with a cargo of crude rubber and Brazil nuts, prompting Vargas to request protective convoys and artillery from the US.[2] It was clear that cargos of strategic materials from Brazil would need military protection.

When the US Navy's PBY5A aircraft of Patrol Wing 11's VP-83 landed in Natal, Brazil was still publicly a neutral country, but was also beginning to be more cooperative with US air forces. The degree of cooperation increased rapidly as the U-boats began sinking Brazilian ships in the south Atlantic. Within five weeks of arriving at Parnamirim, VP-83 was protecting ships from attacks from Axis U-boats. Adm. Karl Dönitz (of the German navy) had shifted a number of both German and Italian U-boats into the south Atlantic to intercept the merchant vessels bring-

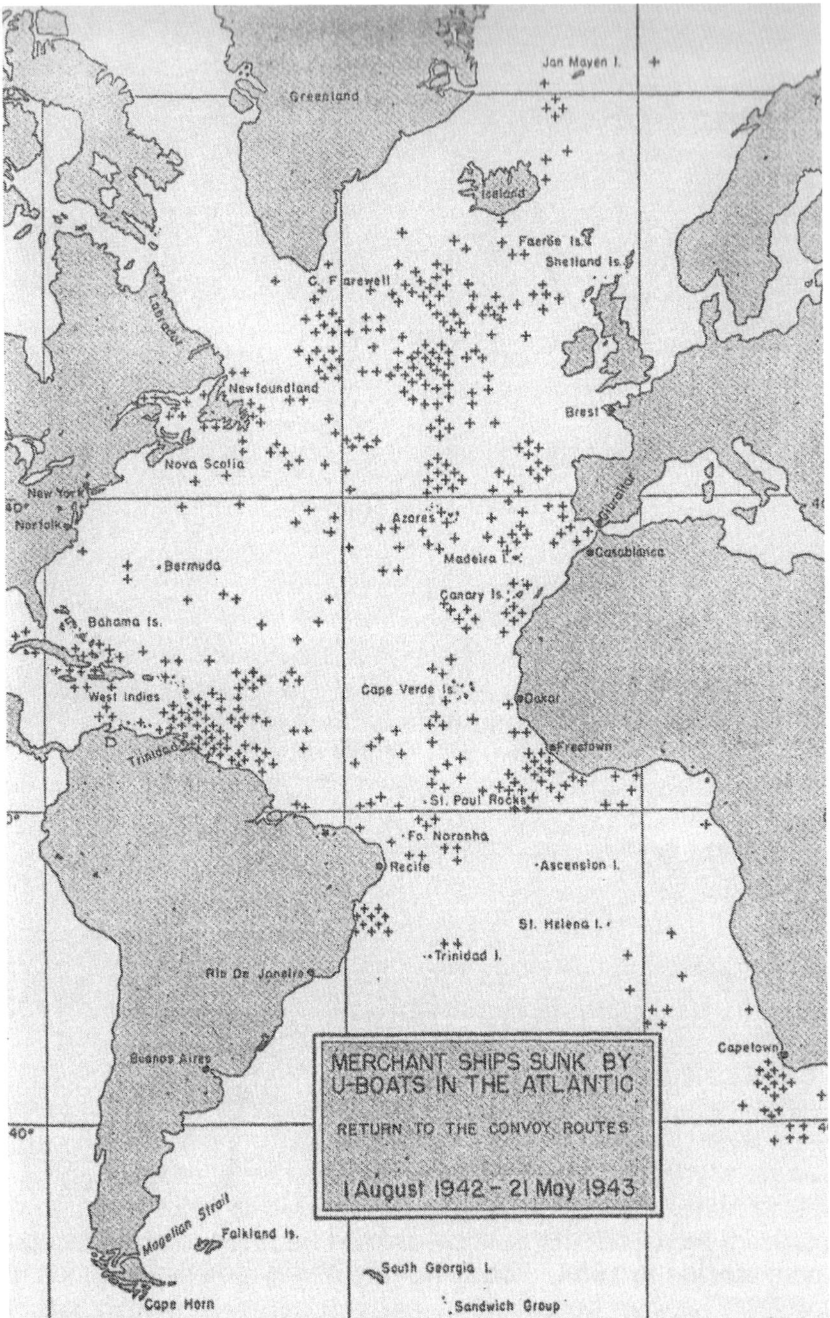

Map of Merchant Ships Sunk by U-boats in the Atlantic. *Courtesy of Fairwing Brazil: Tales of the South Atlantic, by John R. Harrison*

PBY on the Tarmac, Parnamirim 1943. *Courtesy of Fairwing Brazil: Tales of the South Atlantic, by John R. Harrison*

ing supplies from South America, and far Eastern countries to the US and Great Britain. From May 1942 to July 1943, the pace of U-boat activities in the South Atlantic was to grow to its maximum level.[3]

The US government funded Parnamirim, and it was the largest airbase outside of the US. Roads, housing, and sanitation facilities were all needed to accommodate the rapid population explosion in the area, and hundreds of Brazilians migrated to the area to find work. Brazilian soldiers were also sent to the army and navy bases in the area for training.

On 11 December 1941, just four days after the Japanese bombed Pearl Harbor, a US naval unit composed of nine PB4 Catalina and one *Clemson*-class destroyer, arrived in Natal. Two weeks later, fifty marines arrived, to patrol the bases: the US military was now firmly in control of Brazil's northeastern coast. During the course of the war, it is estimated that between three thousand and five thousand Americans were stationed in Parnamirim, and tens of thousands of American and British troops passed through Natal in transit.

Following the war, older residents in Natal told stories to their children and grandchildren about their association with the American troops based in Natal. One story told to me by a taxi driver in Natal, said how the American troops wanted Turkeys for their Thanksgiving dinner, but at the time, Turkeys were not easily available in Brazil. He told me how he and his cousin went to the Natal landfill and killed several Turkey vultures,

Crew of VB-107-B-10. *Courtesy of Fairwing Brazil: Tales of the South Atlantic, by John R. Harrison*

John Harrison in Winter Flying Gear. *Courtesy of Fairwing Brazil: Tales of the South Atlantic, by John R. Harrison*

dressed them and sold them to the US troops for their Thanksgiving celebrations. When asked what the Americans thought about the "Turkeys," the driver said, "they said it was the worst turkey they had ever eaten."

As part of the overall plan of cooperation in the war effort, Brazil would not only become one of the Allies' most important sources of rubber, under new accords signed by President Roosevelt and the government of Getúlio Vargas, the Brazilian government would also send an expeditionary force to join the Allies in Italy. The fact that Brazilian soldiers fought with Eisenhower in Europe is little known by those outside of Brazil itself. In Rio, there are commemorative flags indicating that the Allies in World War II were the US, Great Britain, France and Brazil. The Russian flag is conveniently absent.

Pracinhas Monument in Rio de Janeiro. *Fernando Dall'Acqua, 2005*

During the writing of this book, I received a phone call from John R. (Jack) Harrison, one of the surviving military men who spent most of the war years in Natal, Brazil, as part of a US naval air force photography unit. *New York Times* correspondent Larry Rohter, a specialist on contemporary Brazilian affairs, had referred Jack to me. Knowing of our interest in the US and Brazil's relationship during the turn of the century through the rubber boom, and into World War II, Larry thought Jack and I would have a lot to talk about.

Jack told me about an amazing book he wrote entitled *Fairwing Brazil: Tales of the South Atlantic*. Jack's book provides in graphic detail, with over two hundred seventy-five photographs, the history of the US and Brazilian wartime relationship from 1941 to1947. Jack's book covers information that only someone who lived the story could know.

Recife, which had the requisite harbor facilities, was the main base for the surface ships of the Fourth Fleet which consisted of destroyers, cruisers, service vessels, and eventually (1944–1945) Jeep aircraft carriers. Ibura field at Recife also became the second largest Brazilian-US airbase, and was used by squadrons from both countries. Ultimately, Fairway 16 had joint air bases all the way from Belém in the north, down to Florianopolis in southernmost Brazil, with some of the bases being strictly for seaplanes.

Downtown Natal from Cidade Alta, December 1943. *Courtesy of Fairwing Brazil: Tales of the South Atlantic, by John R. Harrison*

Parnamirim after Full Construction, 1944. *Courtesy of Fairwing Brazil: Tales of the South Atlantic, by John R. Harrison*

Natal also subsequently became the southernmost point for the transit of airplanes, personnel, and wartime materiel to US Allies in Europe,

President Roosevelt and Getúlio Vargas. *Courtesy of Fairwing Brazil: Tales of the South Atlantic, by John R. Harrison*

the Mediterranean, the China-Burma-India, and Pacific war theatres. Accordingly, the US Army Air Force Ferry Command, later the Air Transport Command (ATC) made Natal the "Crossroads of the World," starting in 1942. Many thousands of Allied armed forces personnel (as well as USA celebrity entertainers, and political personages) passed through Natal and the Parnamarim Air Base after it was greatly expanded in 1942–1943.[4]

One of the most notable visits occurred on 28 January 1943, when President Roosevelt arrived in Natal on his way back from the Casablanca conference with Winston Churchill. Roosevelt had notified President Vargas about his itinerary via Natal, so the two leaders seized the opportunity to meet again. At this meeting, Vargas agreed to send three divisions of Brazilian infantry, and a fighter plane squadron to the European theater.[5]

Clear evidence of the good personal relationship between Vargas and Roosevelt, and Admiral Ingram, is obvious in the relaxed demeanor of all present in this photo.[6]

Although World War II was certainly considered a disastrous event, from many perspectives, for Brazil it proved to be a benefit in many ways.

Award Given to Gary Neeleman for His Fair and Reliable Reporting of the Military Coup of 1964. *Gary Neeleman Collection*

The accords with the US, which helped to provide Brazil with a well-equipped military, a string of critical air bases through Brazil, specifically in the Amazon basin, including Belém and Manaus, as well as Natal, brought Brazil literally into the twentieth century, and helped consolidate their vast area into a single nation. Certainly, the US investment in Brazil was unprecedented, and there was some concern that the US would want to continue to have some influence over Brazil and its politics.

In later years, Brazilian military men who served with US troops in Italy, Parnamarim, and other US air bases in Brazil during the war, became staunch friends of the US. Many of them attended US military schools and academies including West Point. During the 1964 military coup in Brazil, these pro-US generals received US military moral support. As a young reporter for United Press International (UPI) in 1964, and responsible for a good portion of the UPI coverage of the coup, I became personally acquainted with many of the military figures involved.

The São Paulo Journalists Organization subsequently awarded me a silver medal for "fair and reliable" coverage of the military coup. For several months my UPI bureau office in São Paulo was under strict military censorship, with two military censors reading all of our dispatches. Even later, after they had withdrawn the censors, our dispatches were closely monitored for many months, until the coup felt it was firmly in control.

In my many conversations and interviews with Brazilian military officers, involved in the coup, they unanimously expressed their respect for the US military leaders they got to know personally during the time they were in Italy under Gen. Eisenhower in World War II.

CHAPTER 6
THE RIO CONFERENCE

As the United States (US) became fully engaged in World War II, a critical conference was called in the early part of January 1942, to be held in Rio de Janeiro. A little over a year earlier, in a conference held in Washington, DC, involving the twenty-one Latin American republics, President Roosevelt quoted Alexandre Dumas in the story of *The Three Musketeers* as, "one for all, all for one." Roosevelt was referring to the defense of the American hemisphere in light of the events in Europe. Although the US was not yet involved in the war, it became evident that there was a real possibility that this would be the case, and the Roosevelt administration was determined to lay the groundwork for the ultimate defense of North and South America.

Nine years earlier, Roosevelt had launched the "Good Neighbor" policy for the Latin American region, and the only possible dissenter to this policy appeared to be the government of Argentina. Argentina had always considered itself as the logical leader of the Southern Hemisphere, and had for many years a rather rocky relationship with not only the US, but also Brazil on its northern border.

The conference in Rio de Janeiro was considered by the Roosevelt administration as a critical test of the US influence in Latin America, and many felt its success or failure could determine the outcome of the war.

The two most important individuals in this historic conference were Sumner Welles, Under Secretary of State in the Roosevelt administration, and Oswaldo Aranha, Brazil's shrewd and very able foreign minister. As an indication of the importance of this conference, Welles arrived in Rio

Sumner Welles

Enrique Ruiz Guiñazú. *Photo in public domain*

with a forty-six-person delegation. Welles had done his homework and was confident that he had the support of the majority of the Latin America republics, and his plan was to convince them that all he needed was their support and that the US would assume the responsibility of defending the hemisphere.

The one question mark in this whole strategy was Argentina, represented by Enrique Ruiz Guiñazú, who was president of the League of Nations Council and carried considerable prestige into the conference.

Fortunately, for the US, Brazil's Oswaldo Aranha believed fervently that close ties with the US were in Brazil's long-term interest. Aranha was considered one of Brazil's most able and colorful diplomats, and had an interesting past as a one-time revolutionary, among other things. He was involved in bringing Vargas to power in 1930 and although he differed considerably with Vargas' totalitarian views, he became Vargas' most influential ally in the long run. He believed in democracy, and his fondness for the US evolved during his time as the Brazilian Ambassador to the US in Washington in 1934.

Like many other successful Brazilian politicians, Oswaldo Aranha was born in the State of Rio Grande do Sul, 15 February 1894, and was raised on his father's cattle ranch. Like other gauchos, Aranha was a zealous patriot and was a critical asset for Getúlio Vargas during his years in power.

Oswaldo Aranha. *Photo in public domain*

Aranha was the host for the conference and also the conference administrator, so he held a position of extraordinary influence. Not only did he have to balance the discussions among the various members of the conference, but he had to also find a way to put forth the US agenda, which could ultimately satisfy the majority, if not all of the representatives.

Probably the main objective of the US strategy was to secure products and goods from Latin America for the war effort. With the Japanese now controlling most rubber supplies from Southeast Asia, it was essential that the US had access to the Latin American products, especially rubber from the Brazilian Amazon. In other words, it was a "goods" not "gold" strategy, which, hopefully their Brazilian friend, Oswaldo Aranha would push for them. Among the essential products the US and the Allies required were rubber, iron ore, chemicals, industrial diamonds, and hemp. Rubber was paramount among these products and Brazil itself was the answer to the rubber shortage.

Jefferson Caffery, US Ambassador to Brazil at the time, was living in Rio de Janeiro and worked alongside Oswaldo Aranha in preparing for the conference. Sumner Welles was well aware of the possibility that the Argentine government would resist the US initiative, but his experience, as the former first secretary in the US embassy in Buenos Aires during the last two years of the World War I, gave him an understanding of the Argentine mentality that he wouldn't have had otherwise. It was partly through his influence that Argentina remained neutral during the World War I.

Even though the majority of Argentina's population was pro-US, Ruiz Guiñazú, with his Spanish ancestry, tended to be anti-US and struggled with the US agenda for political and economic reasons.

The greetings of the delegates took place in the newly refurbished Itamaraty Palace, but the meetings themselves were held in the historic Tiradentes Palace. Tiradentes was a revolutionary and a popular dentist, which accounts for his name "tooth puller" in early Brazilian history. The Portuguese hanged Tiradentes, and then sent his body parts to various parts of Brazil as a warning against other dissenters.

As early as February 1941, the US was eager to set up a conference to determine the attitudes of the Latin American republics toward the possible US involvement in the war. Although they wanted the meeting, as early as possible, US government officials felt it would not be wise for the US to call the meeting, rather they hoped one of the other Latin American republics would call the meeting. As the possibility of the US becoming involved in the war, loomed ever closer, the US government became more and more anxious for such a gathering. Just two days after the bombing of Pearl Harbor, on 9 December 1941, the US got their wish. Chilean foreign minister, Juan B. Rossetti, sent a telegram to the governing board of the Pan American Union asking that a foreign minister meeting be held as soon as possible.

The US moved quickly to agree with Minister Rossetti's proposal and began preparations for such a meeting, which all agreed should be held in the Brazilian capital city of Rio de Janeiro. Among the objectives the US hoped to accomplish in such a meeting was to convince the Latin American republics to sever relations with the Axis powers, even though they may not declare war on the Axis powers. The US's main concern was how Brazil, Chile, Argentina, and Mexico would react to US pressure. The US ambassador to Argentina, Ambassador Norman Armour had warned Sumner Welles that it was becoming more and more certain that the Argentines would not break relations with the Axis. Part of the reason was because of the large number of Italians and Germans that lived in Argentina. The US decided that they would be satisfied if Chile, Mexico and Brazil joined the other Latin American republics in breaking relations with the Axis powers, and that Argentina could go it alone. The other objective, the US hoped to accomplish, was to secure goods and products from the Latin American republics to aid the US in the war effort.

In spite of the fact that the US was not successful in getting Argentina to go along with all of the things they had hoped to achieve, the rest of the Latin American republics, including Brazil, Chile and Mexico went along with the proposals. It was clear that many of the smaller republics were not strong enough to oppose the US pressure, but the fact that the US was ready and willing to protect the hemisphere from Axis incursion, and at the same time buy their products, which would contribute to the US war effort made it possible for an almost unanimous vote.

Obviously, the most important country in Latin America for the US was Brazil. Prior to the US involvement in the war, Getúlio Vargas had vacillated between the US and the Germany, but Brazilian Foreign Minister, Oswaldo Aranha, made the difference and convinced Vargas that the US had more to offer Brazil in the long run than did Germany. Fearing Argentina's reaction, President Vargas wavered about publicly breaking relations with the Axis powers until Aranha threatened to resign and explain his reasons publicly if Brazil did not immediately sever relations with Japan, Germany and Italy.[1] Vargas finally agreed. Aranha's unwavering support for an alliance with the US won the confidence of Undersecretary Welles, who became the leading advocate for protecting Brazil's sovereignty in the Roosevelt administration.

Another part of Vargas' bargain with the US government, was that he signed an agreement on 3 March 1942, which gave the US the right to exploit the natural rubber resources in the Amazon basin. This agreement was known as "the accord," and became a significant contribution to the Allied victory. Vargas for years had been trying to find a way to move Brazilians living in the drought stricken northeastern coast to the Amazon basin to not only secure Brazil's claim on the area, but to also encourage development in the region. The accord between the Vargas government and the Roosevelt administration allowed Vargas to pursue his plan, and fulfill his obligation to the US.

The other elements of the bargain with the US included a string of US airbases along the Brazilian eastern coast, equipment and training for the Brazilian armed forces, and a Vargas agreement to send twenty-five thousand Brazilian troops to Italy to fight alongside the Allies, including an aircraft fighter squadron. There were other economic considerations as well, including the funding of an iron ore or steel operation in northern Brazil. All of this amounted to a deal, which Vargas could not refuse.

CHAPTER 7

THE UNITED STATES-BRAZIL ACCORDS

The United States (US) and Brazil had already established some informal agreements before the outset of the war, but when the Japanese bombed Pearl Harbor on 7 December 1941, both sides moved quickly to formalize these cooperation agreements, particularly those involving rubber production in the Amazon basin. Up to this point, Amazonian rubber was harvested by Brazilians and marketed by the Brazilian rubber elite. Now, for the first time, with the new US Brazilian accords in place, the Brazilian government became involved with a foreign government in the harvesting and marketing of the rubber. Barely two weeks after the Rio conference, the US and Brazilian governments exchanged a preliminary agreement on not only rubber production, but the mechanism by which the US would purchase Brazilian rubber. The two coun-

The Washington Accords. *Chabloz: from the archives of the Universidade Federal do Ceará Museum of Art*

Departing to the Amazon—Engineers in Suits. *Foto Aba-Film: from the archives of the Universidade Federal do Ceará Museum of Art*

tries agreed to establish the Rubber Reserve Company, a US agency that would have offices in Rio de Janeiro, and Washington, DC, and would be responsible for the purchase of all Brazilian rubber, which was not necessary for Brazilian domestic use.

The Brazilian government created a new official organization with the responsibility of investigating and managing strategic resources in the country. They also requested technical assistance from the US to help in this new endeavor. The notes exchanged between the Brazilian Finance Minister, Souza Costa, and the US Acting Secretary of State, Sumner Welles, explained that Brazil required hundred million dollars to put the program into effect. Welles replied the same day that the US was in agreement with the Brazilian proposal, and that the US was prepared to immediately setup a one hundred million dollars line of credit to finance the Brazilian new development organization.

As Sumner Welles negotiated not only with the Brazilian government, but also the US administration in an effort to find common ground for the critical accords, he was very sensitive to Brazil's resistance to the idea that the US would be telling Brazil what to do. In fact, in a memorandum to US Vice President Henry Wallace, he said that he would never approve a policy, "which could only have been interpreted by the Brazilian government, and by the Brazilian people, as an effort to utilize the present international emergency as a means of obtaining from Brazil, rights and prerogatives which would have been tantamount to direct economic intervention in Brazil in derogation of Brazilian sovereignty."[1] Welles had an ally in secretary of commerce Jesse Jones, and together they approved the formation of a Brazilian Development Organization, which would be financed by the US with a credit line of one hundred million dollars. This organization would also oversee the distribution and allocation of the five million dollars, which was promised in the 3 March accords for the development of rubber production in the Amazon.

The following is the actual agreement establishing the Rubber Reserve Company:

• • • • •

NEGOTIATIONS CONCERNING THE PRODUCTION, PURCHASE, AND DISTRIBUTION OF BRAZILIAN RUBBER AND RUBBER PRODUCTS

832.6176/171: Telegram
The Secretary of State to the Ambassador in Brazil (Caffery)[2]
Washington, 9 February 1942, 0000 Hours

313. Your 283, 29 January 2300 Hours.[3] The following from Rubber Reserve:[4]

Rubber Reserve will agree to buy all available rubber until 30 June 1944, at a base price of thirty nine cents f.o.b (free on board). Belém for acre fine, on a washed and dried basis, with appropriate differentials for unwashed types and lower grades.

The above agreement is subject to the following conditions: (1) Assurance from the Brazilian Government that it will put forth utmost effort to encourage production and flow of rubber from all Brazilian markets to the Rubber Reserve Company; (2) Export licenses to be restricted to Rubber Reserve or its nominees: (3) All rubber produced to be sold to the Rubber Reserve on above price basis, except amount required for domestic consumption; and (4) The base price of thirty nine cents f.o.b. Belém with similar differentials is to be established by Brazilian Government for domestic consumption.

Rubber Reserve Company will establish representation in such Brazilian markets as may be necessary to expedite purchases and flow of rubber to the US.

In view of existing conditions affecting rubber supplies, please confer appropriate government officials and advise early as possible.

With reference to (2) above the Priorities Division of the War Production Board on 23 January last issues an order[5] restricting the sale of rubber by dealers to Rubber Reserve Company and conversely restricting purchase of rubber in the US to Rubber Reserve Company. Accordingly, so far as the US is concerned, the necessary machinery has already been established.

HULL

Once the two governments had agreed on the terms of this preliminary agreement, this formal understanding between the two countries became the basis of cooperation for rubber production throughout the duration of the World War II. From the files of the US Senate, we read:

• • • • •

The Brazilian Minister of Finance to the Acting Secretary of State[6]
[translation]
Embassy of the United States of Brazil
Washington, 3 March 1942

Mr Acting Secretary of State:

I have had the honor to exchange notes with Your Excellency today referring to the creation of a Brazilian development organization to which a credit of one hundred million dollars will be extended by the Export-Import Bank. This Brazilian organization has been established in consonance with resolution II of the Third Consultative Meeting of Ministers of Foreign Affairs of the American Republics at Rio de Janeiro, in virtue of which the Brazilian Government resolved to collaborate with the said republics in the greatest possible degree for the immobilization of their economic resources with a view especially to increasing the production of strategic materials essential to the defense of the hemisphere against armed aggression to the maintenance of the economy of Brazil and of other American republics. One of the concrete projects with respect to the development of the sources of Brazil which has been discussed between Your Excellency's Government and the Brazilian Economic Mission, which I have the honor to head, is the one relating to the increase of the production of rubber in the Amazon Valley and adjacent regions. Our discussions on this subject have now reached the stage where I believe it is possible to suggest the following points for the said project:

1. The Rubber Reserve Company, in order to cooperate with the Brazilian Government in the development of rubber in the Amazon Valley and adjacent regions, will establish a fund of five million dollars to be used to increase the production of rubber in said valley and regions. It is to be hoped that the expenditure of this sum will result in the increase of exportation of the Brazilian rubber to the United States of America (USA), in an annual volume of not less than twenty-five thousand tons.

2. The Bank of Brazil or other department or agency of the Brazilian Government will become the sole and final purchaser of rubber, both for exportation and for domestic consumption with the exception of the Rubber Reserve Company, which, in accord with the Bank of Brazil, will be able to purchase rubber for its own account. The Brazilian Government, after reserving quantities adequate for its domestic needs will establish export quotas with a view to furnishing to the USA the greatest quantity of rubber.

3. The Rubber Reserve Company will make a five-year agreement with the Bank of Brazil or other department or agency of the Brazilian government for the acquisition of rubber produced in Brazil.

4. The Rubber Reserve Company will cooperate with the Instituto Agronômico do Norte in the solution of the scientific problems of the development of rubber production in the Amazon Valley and adjacent regions.

5. The Brazilian Government will cooperate fully with the Government of the USA to increase the production of crude and manufactured rubber in Brazil.

6. In compliance with resolution XXX approved in the Consultative Meeting of Ministers of Foreign Affairs of the American Republics held at Rio de Janeiro the Government of the USA will furnish the services of the Division of Health and Sanitation established by the office of the Coordinator of Inter-American Affairs for the development works of the Amazon Valley and adjacent regions, with the objective of carrying out there a program of improvement of sanitary conditions in collaboration with official agencies of other American republics.

In the name of the Brazilian Government and in accordance with the understandings, which the Brazilian Economic Mission reached with representatives of the Government of the USA, I have the honor to request Your Excellency to be good enough to give consideration to the above-mentioned proposals.

I would avail myself of the opportunity to present to your Excellency the assurances of my highest consideration.

A. DE SOUZA COSTA
His Excellency
Sumner Welles
Acting Secretary of State
of the United States of America

That same day, Roosevelt's, acting secretary of State, Summer Welles sent the following acceptance letter to A. De Souza Costa:

• • • • •

The Acting Secretary of State to the Brazilian Minister of Finance[8]
Department of State

Washington
3 March 1942
EXCELLENCY:

I acknowledge the receipt of your note of 3 March 1942 outlining a program for the development of the rubber in the Amazon Valley and adjacent regions as a project for further economic cooperation between the US and the Brazil in furtherance of Resolution II of the Third Meeting of the Ministers of Foreign Affairs of the American Republics at Rio de Janeiro.

I am pleased to inform you that the appropriate agency of the Government of the US have considered this proposal and is prepared to undertake this development in accordance with the specific proposals with respect thereto mentioned in your note.

I believe this program will be a substantial step forward in developing mutually advantageous economic relations between our two countries as contemplated by the Resolution adopted at the conference at Rio de Janeiro.

Accept, Excellency, the assurances of my most distinguished consideration.

Sumner Welles

Acting Secretary of State of the United States of America
His Excellency
Dr Arthur de Souza Costa
Minister of Finance of Brazil

An agreement between the Government of the US and the Brazilian Government for increasing the production of rubber in Brazil was effected by exchange of notes between the Under Secretary of State (Welles) and the Brazilian Minister of Finance (Souza Costa), signed at Washington, 3 March 1942. For texts of notes, see Department of State Executive Agreements Series No. 371, or 57 Stat. (pt. 2) 1318.

Unfortunately, the Brazilian delegation did not include a rubber expert and the Commercial Association of Para and Amazonas were quick to criticize the Souza Costa delegation for agreeing to what they perceived as a guaranteed bargain price of thirty-nine cents per pound FOB (Free on Board) Belém for the highest quality (Acre fina) crude rubber exports bound for the US. This price was considerably higher than the 18.5 cents per pound that the US paid for Asian crude rubber in 1941, before the Japanese occupied Southeast Asia, but Amazonian rubber elites thought that a higher price could be extracted due to the exigencies of war.[9] In spite of their complaints, the guaranteed price was high enough for the Amazonian elites to go into rubber production.

Valentine Boucas, who had been representing rubber companies in Brazil, was named by Vargas, as the President of the Brazilian commission to control the Washington accords. Vargas trusted Boucas to negotiate effectively with the key people in the Roosevelt administration, including Nelson Rockefeller, who Vargas thought might have undermined Brazil's sovereignty over the Amazon. There are those who felt the Amazon should be under international control and Vargas was aware of this. The good neighbor policy was fully accepted by Roosevelt and acting secretary of State Welles' defense of Brazil's sovereignty helped the US obtain Vargas' approval for moderate rubber prices.

The US secretary of commerce was designated to examine, monitor, and approve through the Import Export Bank all financing of projects working in conjunction with the Brazilian government. In spite of these official documents, signed by representatives of both governments, for years there has been a question in the minds of many Brazilians as to whether or not the US government paid for the rights to exploit Brazilian rubber as described in the 3 March 1942 accords.

Over the last few years, as we visited the city of Porto Velho, in the state of Rondônia, in the Amazon basin, the question of payment by the US has been continually raised. The Rubber Tappers Union lawyer, Irlan da Silva, has been persistent in asking us, and many others, to verify if the US actually provided Brazil with the one hundred million dollars line of credit mentioned in the accord, and the five million dollars additional to increase rubber production, and provide sanitary and healthcare facilities. In addition, they are asking for verification that the US paid the thirty-nine cents per pound established by the Brazilian government as the price of the rubber itself. This money, in turn should have compensated the rubber tappers and their families. We visited with Irlan da Silva several times in Porto Velho, and many of the surviving rubber tappers now in their nineties, and older. One individual we spoke to was one hundred seven years old, and is still asking when he will be paid. The majority of these old survivors live in a small favela (slum) on the outskirts of Porto Velho.

In 2010, we traveled to Brasilia and met Irlan da Silva there and introduced him to the new American ambassador, Thomas Shannon, where we explained the current dilemma faced by the Rubber Tappers Union concerning US payment to the Brazilian government. Irlan da Silva explained that Brazilian President Ignacio Lula da Silva had indirectly recognized that the rubber tappers had more compensation coming and ordered a symbolic increase in their monthly pension. However, he refused to admit that the US had paid for the rubber and, according to Irlan da Silva, Lula alluded to the fact that the Brazilian government had not received full payment from the US for the rubber. We showed ambassador Shannon copies of the original 3 March 1942 accord, and other subsequent agreements pertaining to the organization of the Rubber Reserve Corporation and the details of subsequent payments to the Brazilian government. Ambassador Shannon was very interested in the copies of the transactions and said he was not aware of any request by the Rubber Tappers Union for an explanation as to how and when the US paid the Brazilian government.

Avenue Showing the Theater, Ideal Club, and Park in Manaus. *National Archives Building, Washington, DC (NAB)*

Later the same day, we met with Brazilian foreign minister Antonio Patriota, and he also told us he was not aware of the details regarding the financial transactions between the two countries, but would be interested in knowing more.

Part of the intent of this book is to not only record the history of the rubber tappers contribution to World War II, but to also trace, through newly revealed documents from the files of the US senate the money trail from the US government to the Brazilian government and Brazilian banks.

After the signing of the US-Brazil accords in March 1942, President Roosevelt assigned responsibility for the rubber production program in Latin America to the Rubber Reserve Company, a subsidiary of the US Reconstruction Finance Corporation (RFC). The Rubber Development Corporation (RDC) succeeded the Rubber Reserve Company in early 1943. Nelson Rockefeller's Coordinator of Inter-American Affairs (CIAA) was removed from direct involvement in rubber production and then given primary responsibility for public health and sanitation, as well as public information and wartime propaganda.

With the direct involvement of the US and all of its influence and power, the question arises, why weren't the health care services for the rubber tappers more successful? The answer lies in the difficulty in providing food and health services to tens of thousands of isolated rubber tappers who lived and worked dispersed throughout a vast region of dense rainforests, and hundreds of tributaries, some of which were inaccessible for months due to seasonal variations in river depths.[10]

The RDC established its headquarters in Manaus in the historic and opulent Amazonas Theater and worked under the direction of Phillip Williams. The RDC established branch offices in strategic port towns of the Western Amazon, including Benjamin Constant Boca Do Acre, Guajará-Mirim, Joao Pessoa, Porto Velho, Rio Branco, Sena Madureira and Villa Feijo.

Williams dispatched twenty North American and fifteen Brazilian rubber technicians to far-flung tributaries to report on conditions in the rubber estates and obstacles to increasing production. RDC field technicians were instructed to examine all aspects of rubber production including: evaluation of rubber estates and operators; existing and potential production areas; sites available for rubber plantations; status of and requirements for equipment and facilities; production techniques and training needs; labor supply, including competing industries; labor conditions; transportation facilities and needs; marketing procurement; local governments (including legislation, taxes, attitudes of local officials); existing programs of Brazilian agencies; and recommendations for cooperation with other US agencies.[11] This study not only examined the technical problems facing the Amazon rubber industry, but also the social challenges facing the rubber tappers themselves.

The reports of the US experts contributed insights into the economic, social and labor conditions in the Amazonian hinterlands, and were valuable not only for the RDC but also provided the US government with first-hand information and intelligence about the contested Amazonian frontier. In February 1942, Sumner Welles informed Ambassador Jefferson Caffery in Brazil, and other US embassies in Latin America that US rubber experts sent to conduct field surveys in the Amazon had been instructed to accept fact-finding assignments from US military attaches and report to them on their findings.[12]

Rubber technicians criticized the management of the rubber estates on the Tapajós River. Owned by a combination of rubber tappers and small producers, many estates had been neglected for ten to twenty years.

Rubber tappers still used machetes to cut and bleed the bark of the rubber trees for latex, although southeast Asian plantations had increased productivity through the use of the Jebong knife, a more precise tool, shaped like a "J," that increased latex yields without killing the Hevea trees[13] (latex vessels are close to the inner cambium layer, which, if cut, destroy the trees).[14]

Conditions on rubber estates varied depending upon their access to food and supplies, with better conditions prevailing on rivers with easy access to Belém, the main port of entry for food and supplies shipped from Pará, southern Brazil and US. One of the most important variables was the availability of reliable and inexpensive food supplies at the estates. Pará had an important agricultural sector and good distribution networks.[15]

Conditions worsened in the western Amazon and on remote tributaries in other regions where food shortages were chronic, and rubber estates depended on shipments of imported food from southern Brazil or overseas. Beriberi cases were observed among the youngest and most inexperienced rubber soldiers. Incidence of disease and number of deaths was much higher among the migrant rubber soldiers than among indigenous and caboclos rubber tappers.[16]

The following was sent only ten days after the 3 March 1942 accord:

• • • • •

811.20 Defense (M) Brazil/327: Telegram
The Acting Secretary of State to the Ambassador in Brazil (Caffery)[17]
Washington, 13 March 1942, 1900 Hours

640. Following from the Rubber Reserve:

The following agreement was signed by the Rubber Reserve Company and the Republic of Brazil on 3 March:

This Agreement made and entered into as of this 3 March 1942, by and between the Rubber Reserve Company, an Agency of the US Government (hereinafter called "Reserve"), a corporation existing under the laws of the USA and having an office for the transaction of business in Washington, DC party of the first part, and the Republic of Brazil (hereinafter sometimes called "Brazil"). Party of the second part;

WITNESSETH:

1. Brazil agrees to establish, or cause to be established, a single selling agency (which will be the Bank of Brazil or some other Brazilian Government Department or Agency, such selling agency being herein referred to as the "Selling Agency"), located at Belém, Para, and at such other places as may be deemed desirable by Reserve and Brazil, with appropriate authority to acquire and sell crude rubber produced within the territory of the Republic of Brazil (such crude rubber being hereinafter referred to as "Rubber").

2. Reserve agrees to make such arrangements as may be necessary for the purchase of the Rubber, it is understood that all such purchases shall be on the basis of cash against shipping documents, f.o.b. Belém, Para, or such other places as may be deemed desirable by Reserve and Brazil. All of the rubber so purchased shall be subject to a final price adjustment based on quality inspection and net certified weights determined at the port of entry in USA.

3. During the term of this agreement Reserve agrees to buy and Brazil (acting through the Selling Agency) agrees to sell all of the Rubber, which is not required by the Republic of Brazil for domestic consumption or use.

4. Reserve and Brazil agree that the base price for all purchases and sales of the Rubber under paragraph 3 hereof shall be thirty-nine cents, USA currency, per pound f.o.b. Belém, Para, for Upriver Acre Fine, on a washed and dried basis with appropriate differentials for unwashed types and lower grades (said base price, together with said differentials being hereinafter referred to as the "Fixed Price"); provides, however, that after the expiration of the first two years of the term of this agreement the Fixed price shall be subject to such adjustments from time to time as Reserve and Brazil may mutually agree is appropriate by reason of any changed circumstances affecting the world's price of crude rubber. In addition to the base price above referred to, the Rubber Reserve Company will pay premiums as follows; two and half cents per pound for all rubber in excess of five thousand tons and up to ten thousand tons purchased hereunder by the Rubber Reserve Company during any one year of this agreement; a premium of five cents per pound for all rubber purchased hereunder in excess of ten thousand tons during any one year of this agreement all premiums so paid.

(a) Shall be credited against the five million dollars fund of the Rubber Reserve Company referred to in paragraph 1 of the note of His

Excellency, the Brazilian Minister of Finance, addressed to the Acting Secretary of State of the USA, dated 3 March 1942.

(b) Shall be turned over by the Brazilian Government to the Instituto Agronômico do Norte, or other dep artment or agency of the Brazilian Government having similar functions, to be utilized for the immediate expansion of the production and improvement of quality of raw wild rubber in the Amazon Valley and adjacent regions.

It is understood that Brazil intends to establish, or cause to be established, the Fixed Price for all purchases and sales of the Rubber for domestic consumption or use.

5. Brazil agreed that it shall use its best efforts to cause the maximum amount of the Rubber to be produced and to be made available for sale to the Reserve.

6. Brazil recognizing the large requirements of rubber in the US for war emergency, agrees to restrict to the USA, the exportation of the rubber in raw and manufactured form from the Republic of Brazil, provided such arrangements shall be made for the purchase by the US of manufacture rubber at prices to be mutually agreed upon. Reserve agrees that all rubber purchased by it hereunder shall be disposed of only in accordance with the regulations of the War Production Board or some other Agency of the US Government having similar authority.

7. Reserve agrees that it shall use its best efforts to expedite the purchase and exportation of the Rubber, which Reserve is obligated to buy under paragraph 3 hereof.

8. The term of this agreement shall be for a period beginning with the date hereof and ending on 31 December 1946, unless sooner terminated by the mutual consent of the parties hereto. (End of agreement)

Rubber Reserve Company is also prepared to pay the following prices. F.o.b. Belém for the different grades of rubber, and is establishing a letter of credit through the RFC so that the Bank of Brazil may draw against such letter of credit as rubber is shipped from Brazil on ocean going vessels destined for continental US ports:

- Acre Washed: 39 cents
- Upriver Washed: 385/8 cents
- Islands Washed: 385/8 cents
- Acre Cut Classified (Crude): 305/8 cents
- Upriver Cut Classified (Crude): 30¼ cents
- Islands Cut Classified (Crude): 281/8 cents

- Sernamby Rama Washed: 281/8 cents
- Sernamby Rama Crude: 20 cents
- Sernamby Cameta Washed: 295/8 cents
- Sernamby Cameta Crude: 15½ cents
- Cacho Washed: 33½ cents
- Camacho Crude: 24 cents

and Rubber Reserve Company will pay the following prices, USA Currency, per pound, f.o.b. São Salvador (Bahia) and such other Brazilian ocean ports, as Reserve and Brazil may mutually agree upon for the following grades of rubber:

- Ceará Scrap (Crude): 17 cents
- Mangabeira (Crude): 17 cents

Please advise Brazilian Government and Bank of Brazil accordingly. Also advise Rubber Reserve Company if Brazil proposes to provide for shipping arrangements or if Reserve is expected to do so. Suggest Brazilian Government be encouraged to expedite selling arrangements so that exports can be started to US.

Welles

It is interesting to note that in item 2 of this accord above, both countries agreed that rubber purchased by the US would be on a "cash only basis at the shipping point," which dispels any notion that the US did not pay for any rubber they received from the Amazon.

The accords further make clear that payment of money to the rubber tappers for their work and their working conditions was the responsibility of the Brazilian government, not the US. The accords clearly indicate that the US agreed to finance the entire operation for the war effort, and although the US worked closely with the Brazilian government, the ultimate responsibility of the disbursement of all funds was in the hands of the Brazilian banks and government agencies.

As part of the original agreement dated 3 March 1942, the US government expressed specific concern for the health and sanitation conditions in the area where the rubber tappers would be extracting the latex. This concern counted for the additional five million dollars that was included in the original agreement totaling one hundred five million dollars. The government of the US agreed that five million dollars would be made available immediately to finance the infrastructure of the region to enable the rubber tappers to begin work as soon as possible.

The following is the agreement between the USA and the Brazil concerning the health and sanitation program. It was affected by exchange of notes, and signed in Washington, DC, on 14 March 1942:

• • • • •

The Acting Secretary of State to the Brazilian Minister for Finance[18]
Department of State
Washington
14 March 1942

My Dear Mr Minister,

I refer to the note which we exchanged on 3 March 1942 on rubber development in the Amazon Valley, and specifically to Point 6 of your note concerning the readiness of this Government to lend its good offices through the Health and Sanitation Division of the Office of the Coordinator of Inter-American Affairs in matters pertaining to health and sanitation conditions in the Amazon Valley. I refer also to the agreements reached on that day with respect to other economic projects.

The CIAA is prepared to send at once to Brazil, on your request, to cooperate with corresponding officials of the Brazilian Government and its health services, such experts as your Government desires in order to collaborate in developing a specific health and sanitation program. The program would be initially designed for the Amazon basin area for the special purpose of aiding in the stimulation of rubber production, but at the desire of the Government of Brazil could be extended to other areas.

For these purposes this Government, through the agency of the CIAA will provide an amount not to exceed five million dollars to be expanded toward the development of this health and sanitation program. The expenditure of these funds may be applied not only to health and sanitation projects, but also in the discretion of the Government of Brazil, for such medical and sanitation engineering training as the Government of Brazil may wish undertaken by Brazilian specialists.

It is understood that the Government of Brazil will furnish such expert personnel, materials, services and funds for local expenditures, as it may consider necessary for the efficient development of the program.

The group of US medical and sanitation specialists, which the Brazilian Government indicates should be sent by the office of the CIAA, shall be under the direction of the chief medical officer of that Office who will in turn be under the supervision of the appropriate officials of the Brazilian Government.

(not signed)

CHAPTER 8
THE RUBBER RESERVE COMPANY

The primary responsibility of the Rubber Reserve Company was to find rubber wherever it might be. In order to do this, the US government had to bring in the most able field scientists available to search out latex bearing plants at their source, anywhere in the world, and determine which would be the best. The Amazon's Hevea brasiliensis was, obviously, the best source, which produced Para Fine, named after the Brazilian province where the trees were found. But there were also latex bearing trees in Colombia, Bolivia, Peru, the Congo, Mexico, the Dutch West Indies, and India, among others.

Undoubtedly, one of the most knowledgeable young botanists recruited was Harvard educated Richard Evans Schultes, who was hired on 20 November 1942. He was sent immediately to the Amazon via Colombia where he was told by the Rubber Reserve representative in Colombia, Jules de Wael Mayer, a Dutchman from the West Indies, that he should investigate three vast concessions owned by three wealthy Colombian families. Schultes located the three concessions of forest-land after much effort and started his quest for latex. After weeks of exploring the concessions, he found that the trees were not large enough, or plentiful enough to warrant commercial exploitation. What Schultes found was that the logistics alone made it nearly impossible to exploit the latex bearing trees in this area.

According to Wade Davis in his book, *One River*: "Caught between the bureaucrats in Washington and a small band of explorers was the old Dutchman, known always to the men as Mr Mayer. A portly figure well past retirement age, Mayer had worked for years in the plantations of the far east. Posted to Bogota as senior field technician, he had taken on the task not only of maximizing Colombian rubber production, but of insulating his men from the whims and idiocies of his superiors back in Washington. For that he had earned the affection of all those working with him."

Although Mayer wanted the rubber development program to work in Colombia and Brazil, by the end of 1943, he had serious doubts of its viability. Mayer was fiercely loyal to his men, but began to wonder if the program would, in the end, be worth the risks these men were taking.

Schultes and other explorers came up with reports that indicated that the Apaporis River area could produce three thousand tons of rubber a year, but, Mayer concluded, it would take near ten thousand men to reach this goal, and where would these men come from? And even if he did succeed, how significant would the contribution be? The numbers simply did not add up. The Amazon supported an estimated three hundred million Hevea trees, theoretically enough to yield eight hundred thousand tons of rubber a year. But these trees were scattered over millions of square miles of forest, with a density of perhaps one tree per acre. Even at the height of the boom, when prices rose as high as three dollars a pound, and tens and thousands of rubber tappers spread through the Amazon, the total annual harvest for all of South America never surpassed fifty thousand tons. Industrial America alone consumed fourteen times that amount each year.[1]

Without a doubt, the natural rubber produced in the Amazon basin helped bridge the increasing demand for natural rubber for the war effort at a critical time, but in the long run, there would have to be another solution.

Four days after Pearl Harbor, the US government initiated a recycling program for scrap rubber of all kinds. People were encouraged to search their neighborhoods for old tires and tubes, and over four hundred thousand gas stations were designated as collection points for this used rubber. In spite of all of these efforts, the supply of rubber in the Allied countries continued to dwindle. In 1941, the US imported over a million tons of natural rubber, but by 1943, only fifty-five thousand three hundred twenty-nine tons of natural rubber were imported.

Although scrap rubber also began to play an important role in meeting the rising demand, it was soon determined that scrap rubber also had to have a one part natural rubber to ten parts scrap mix in order to increase its capacity.

The development of synthetic rubber in the US was still in its infancy. The first synthetic rubber was developed by Dupont in 1932, but was still sadly inferior to natural rubber for essential products such as tires and tubes. It was also considerably more expensive than natural rubber at that time. When it became apparent at the end of 1943, that unless synthetic rubber became available in huge quantities, the war effort could fail. At this point, the US realized that its back was against the wall, and at a cost of nearly six hundred seventy three million dollars they pulled off one of the most amazing scientific and engineering feats of all time. Only the Manhattan Project, the development of the atomic bomb, may have been more significant.

It did not take long for the use of synthetic rubber to become an essential element, not only in the war effort, but also in the domestic area and post war period. In spite of its usefulness, in order to be reliable, synthetic rubber required a mix of natural rubber. As the men who made the tires used to say, "synthetic rubber is a great material. It will mix in any proportion, and the more natural rubber you put in, the better it is." Because of the fact that synthetic and scrap rubber still did not solve the problem entirely, rubber from Brazil remained a significant priority. Even today, airplane tires are one hundred percent natural rubber as are the sidewalls of automobile tires, as synthetic rubber does not have the resilience or strength of natural rubber.

With the formal agreements in place, financing arranged, a plan for the improvement of health and sanitation conditions, and the Rubber Reserve Company ready to buy all available Brazilian rubber for the war effort, the Brazilian government was ready to begin recruiting the rubber tappers who would extract the precious latex.

Up to this point, dating back to the turn of the century, the rubber elite of the Amazon ruled the economy of the Amazon with an iron fist. In partnership with regional plantation owners with foreign traders and investors from abroad, Brazil was the rubber capital of the world. In 1900, most all of the rubber in the world came from Brazil, but by 1922, only six percent of the world's rubber came from the Amazon.

When World War II broke out, it was the answer to the dilemma of Brazilian President, Getúlio Vargas. For years, he had tried to find a way

Getúlio Vargas. *National Archives Building, Washington, DC (NAB)*

to integrate the Amazon with the rest of Brazil and the agreements with the Allies, to revive the rubber industry was the ultimate answer.

Vargas had been wrestling with a chronic drought problem in Brazil's northeast and the idea of recruiting thousands of northeasterners to serve in the Amazon as rubber soldiers with the responsibility of extracting thousands of tons of latex for the war effort allowed Vargas to fulfill two of his desired objectives. He would not only be able to profit from the financing of the new rubber initiative in the Amazon, and he would also solve the problems in the northeast.

Although the majority of the rubber soldiers came from the State of Ceará, many also came from the States of Rio Grande do Norte and Paraiba. As health was an important concern to the US, the recruits were carefully examined and as many as ten percent were rejected due to health problems. Many were suffering from small pox, yellow fever, typhoid fever, and tetanus. Although the Vargas' rhetoric sounded convincing about the responsibility and duty to serve the nation in the war effort, in truth the majority of them enlisted out of poverty and lack of opportunity in the Brazilian northeast.

As the US became aware of the Vargas plan to send thousands of northeastern Brazilians to the Amazon, they also became aware of the need to assess the capabilities of these men to tap the rubber. Prior to the Vargas call for the "rubber army," A report from the US Embassy in Rio de Janeiro written in October 1940, reveals that the image of migrant rubber tappers as *flagelados* had not changed since the heyday of the Amazon rubber boom (at the turn of the century). Embassy counselor William Burdett traveled to the Amazon to investigate the potential for increasing rubber production. Assessing the labor situation, he painted a dismal picture of the migrant workers:[2]

> Over a period of one hundred years or more the sertanejo of the semi-arid of northeastern Brazil … has sought the Amazon during the periodic droughts which kill his cattle, dry up his wells and lay waste his fields. He does not abandon the *sertão* (hinterland) until he is driven to it by hunger, thirst and penury … His body is racked by syphilis, leprosy, tuberculosis, and other diseases. His resistance to the new diseases he encounters in the Amazon is almost nil … The government occasionally sends feeble contingents of laborers from Ceará. One group of one hundred seventy arrived at Manaus … They were the most decrepit, undernourished, ineffectual looking individuals one can imagine. Some of the rubber people saw them and said most of them would probably die in the jungle. Obviously, they were picked out as being undesirable labor at their homes.

Through this report, the embassy informed Washington about three obstacles to increasing rubber production that would later hinder the wartime effort: the poor health and physical fitness of indigent migrant workers from the northeast; their vulnerability to new diseases in the Amazon; and the tendency of the government to select unsuitable and undesirable laborers to be transferred to the Amazon.

As a result of this report, in their discussions with the Brazilian government, the USA representatives made it clear that the accords would have to include funding for improved healthcare, better sanitation, and medical services. The Vargas government readily accepted this, and the accord dated 3 March 1942, included a five million dollar advance specifically designated for the improvement of the health and sanitation infrastructure in the rubber tapping estates.

At the same time, rubber estate owners in Amazonas assured the US Consul in Belém that with an adequate labor supply and an assured market for their rubber, they could increase rubber production several times over 1940 levels.[3] "This seemed to satisfy the US officials in Rio de Janeiro.

President Vargas was determined to make his new alliance with the US work, and he spared no opportunity. He enlisted the help of the Catholic Church in the northeast and assigned priests to the rubber soldier contingents to provide spiritual assistance and look after the soldiers' families. He further needed the priests to keep the rubber soldiers in line with religious orientation, moral direction and patriotism.

He assigned Father Helder Camara, a native of Ceará, a well-known charismatic preacher in the region as the Director of Religious Assistance.

In later years, Father Helder Camara moved to São Paulo and became an activist protesting the military regime, which toppled the João Goulart government in 1964. In fact, he published an ultra-leftist newspaper called *Brasil Urgente*. I was in São Paulo at the time working for United Press International (UPI) as a correspondent and covered the 1964 military coup, including the activities of Helder Camara. He later returned to the northeast and the city of Recife where he organized the "Ligas Camponesas" (Peasant Leagues) to protest the military dictatorship and human rights abuses.

As recruiting rubber soldiers progressed, the Brazilian government found that there were many difficulties they had not anticipated. The shear number of recruits that had enlisted for the trip to the Amazon began to overwhelm the Brazilian agency, Servico de Mobilizacao de Trabalhadores para Amazonia (SEMTA), which was set up to receive the recruits and transport them to the rubber fields of the Amazon. In one incident, a group of four hundred rubber soldiers dispatched by train from Piauí to São Luíz do Maranhão were promised a meal at a stop in the town of Caixas. Arriving hungry from traveling all day without food, they were met by the mayor, who informed them there was no food available. The rubber soldiers rioted and invaded the local market, taking food and destroying stalls.[4]

Another benefit of the new World War II rubber program for Vargas was the opportunity to break the back of the old *aviador* trading system controlled by the rubber estate owners. However, efforts by the two governments to break this stranglehold of the Amazonian elite on the rubber trading system and improve conditions on the rubber estates predictably met with resistance. The traditional *aviador* trading system was based on a chain of patron-client relationships through which large Amazonian import-export firms advanced supplies on credit to merchants, and river traders who, in turn, marked them up and delivered them to far-flung rubber estates on credit in return for their future rubber production. Rubber estate owners and managers, in turn, advanced the merchandise to their rubber tappers, debiting their accounts for over-priced imported food and basic supplies and crediting them for their rubber production, which they delivered to the same riverboat traders. Riverboat traders delivered rubber to *aviador* firms, which forwarded the raw material to international exporting companies. Rubber estates and traders profited by overcharging rubber tappers for their food and supplies and undervaluing their rubber production, leaving most rubber tappers in perpetual debt. Disappointingly, low rubber productivity was linked to the abysmal conditions on many estates, where the triple scourges of malnutrition, disease, and chronic poverty plagued the workers, and to complicate the situation further, the *aviador* trading system made it even worse.

After a great deal of study, the US government and the Getúlio Vargas government decided that one way to end the *aviador* system was for the Rubber Development Corporation (RDC) and the Brazilian agency Superintendência de Abastecimento do Vale Amazônico (SAVA) was to provide direct shipments of food stuffs and critical supplies to the rubber estate trading posts. By doing this, they would eliminate the middle-men, or *aviadores,* who profited with higher prices and kept the rubber tappers in financial bondage. The Vargas government agreed with this new concept, but it quickly became evident that the vast disbursement of the rubber estates throughout the Amazon made it almost impossible for the two governments to police or even track the activities of the hundreds of traders that operated, not only on the big rivers, but along the tributaries where many thousands of the rubber tappers worked and lived.

The wartime alliance with Brazil gave the US government an unprecedented opportunity to send technical experts to survey the Amazon and gather information about its society and natural resources, despite wariness on the part of Brazilian nationalists about the post-war intentions of North American business interests.[5]

The Amazon itself is one of the most unusual areas of the world and for the US it was a first time experience for many of the US technicians and engineers. Following the war, there was a great deal of criticism about how the US was unprepared for what they were trying to do in the Amazon. Their equipment was not able to withstand the high humidity and blazing tropical heat. They were completely unprepared for the diseases they encountered, and the food they brought in was not appropriate. In short, it was determined that the US should have consulted a great deal more with their Brazilian counterparts and Brazilian locals in the Amazon region in order to avoid many of the complications and difficulties they encountered.

Walter Walmsley, economic counselor of the US embassy in Rio, on 8 October 1943, produced a scathing report on the rubber business in the Amazon:

> No darker picture exists anywhere of what in more progressive countries we choose to call corruption. Yet, the established society, with its century-old tentacles stretching up all the thousands of tributaries, was totally ignored in our earlier rubber program. The river trade is the bloodstream of this feudal social organization. We have attempted to cut across those arteries expecting that the body would not only survive but would also be useful to us ... We have entered someone else's property and ignored the owner. We have made decisions not only in Belém and Manaus, which is bad enough, but also in Rio and Washington, which is worse, on problems with which we have not the faintest familiarity ... The Amazon is a hierarchy of middlemen feeding on the body of the *seringueiro* ... Cash means little to a *seringueiro* buried in his pest-ridden *barracão* (shack) ... What he needs is food and medicine to keep him alive and alcohol to keep him from despair. What difference is it to him if he gets out of the red and can't eat? If a *seringueiro* is credited with a higher price for his rubber, he is debited with a higher price for his supplies. Neither the Rubber Bank nor the RDC nor any other entity without the river organization of the commercial firms, has anything to offer the *seringueiro* in return for added rubber production.[6] Walmsley concluded that it was a mistake to ignore established trading practice in Amazonian society, "with its century-old tentacles stretching up all the thousands of tributaries."[7]

President Vargas spared no effort in recruiting tens of thousands of northeastern Brazilians to travel from their homes in the northeast to the jungles of the Amazon to participate in what Vargas called a patriotic effort to win the war. He made them feel, in his very aggressive campaign, that they were equal to the Brazilian soldiers serving in the military alongside American soldiers and sailors stationed along the Brazilian northeastern coast, and the 25,000 Brazilian soldiers fighting in the expeditionary force under Gen. Dwight D. Eisenhower in Europe. Ironically, less than 500 Brazilian soldiers lost their lives during the war in Europe, while nearly thirty thousand of the fifty-five thousand rubber soldiers who worked in the Amazon jungle tapping rubber lost their lives.

The recruits were referred to as *arigós* (rugged men). In a comprehensive newspaper report, by journalist, Ariadne Araújo published on 21 June 1998, in *O Povo* daily newspaper in Fortaleza, Ceará, Brazil and

Rubber Tapper. *National Archives Building, Washington, DC (NAB)*

Ariadne describes the recruiting process, where the Vargas government made dazzling promises to the recruits. She tells how they were promised a much better life in the lush jungles, of the Amazon, money that would eventually make them rich and transportation to and from the rubber fields. Vargas also promised that the old system of literal peonage they had heard about from their fathers and grandfathers would not be permitted under the new order. The Cearenses were told they were helping to win the war, which made it different than it was thirty years earlier, prior to the rubber crash of 1913.

During the early rubber boom from the turn of the century, thousands of Cearenses and Brazilians from other parts of Brazil streamed into the Amazon to find work in the rubber fields, with the promise of riches and opportunity. When world rubber production transferred to the British colonies in Southeast Asia, in 1913, Brazil's rubber bubble burst. Many of the rubber plantations and associated enterprises were bankrupt and the Brazilian government itself had no solution to the problem. The once glittering rubber capital of Manaus on the Amazon was ruined, and the workers from the rubber fields were issued tickets to return to their home areas in northeastern Brazil with little or nothing to show for their years of labor in the jungle. With Vargas' glowing promises to the sons and grandsons of those original tappers, it was hoped that this time would be different.

Propaganda. Araújo, Ariadne, *O Povo*, Fortaleza, Ceará, Brazil, Sunday, 21 June 1998.

Among the incentives offered by Vargas was a pair of blue denim jeans, an unbleached cotton top, a straw hat, a pair of boots, a tin mug, a deep plate, a fork, a hammock, and a pack of cigarettes. All of this, plus a burlap bag to carry their personal belonging. This was the uniform of the rubber soldier. Other incentives included the promise of easy money, medical care, and transportation to and from the rubber plantations. These promises appeared throughout the northeast on the propaganda posters printed and posted by the federal government. For an unemployed northeastern farmer who had suffered with one of the worst droughts in history in Ceará, the Vargas offer was very hard to resist. Consequently, an estimated fifty-five thousand men, some with their families enlisted in the rubber army.

In Ariadne's newspaper article, she interviews an old rubber tapper, Joaquim Moreira de Souza, from Russas, west of Ceará, who explained that the drought, the fear of being sent to Europe to fight in the expeditionary force and Vargas' promises made him decide to join the rubber army. Vargas offered other incentives in his rubber campaign: the biggest producer of rubber during the year would win thirty-five thousand *cruzeiros* (currency of the time), including a free three thousand mile trip by truck, train, or boat to "El Dorado."

Although the focus of the recruiting campaign was in Fortaleza, capital of the State of Ceará, the federal government opened recruiting stations throughout the interior of the state, which attracted thousands of unemployed men. All that was required to become a rubber soldier was a cursory physical examination and a signature on a paper. Most of these men were hired on the spot with a salary of fifty US cents a day, and housing facilities during the time they were employed as tappers.

Departing to the Amazon—Waving from the Truck. *Aba-Film: from the archives of the Universidade Federal do Ceará Museum of Art*

Arigós on the Rail. *National Archives Building, Washington, DC (NAB)*

With literally thousands of men joining the ranks of the rubber soldiers in a brief period of time, there was a serious problem of discipline. As a

The *Delaware. National Archives Building, Washington, DC (NAB)*

result, the federal government was forced to initiate a program of military like discipline to keep the men inline.

On the banks of the Amazon River, there is no one that doesn't know the story of the rubber soldiers. Students, fishermen, merchants, and housekeepers: all of these people have a friend or relative that was in the army of rugged men (arigós). They all remember that time which, for them, still hasn't quite ended. In a united order, they received instructions from their bosses. In platoons, they marched through the streets and squares of the city. They bid farewell to Ceará, in a state of euphoria in the bed of a truck. Now, fifty years later, these images still find the rubber soldiers as a living memory, of a premature retirement, and a continuing fight for status, and recognition as heroes of the motherland and for the dignity of her citizens.[8]

In the back of trucks, in cargo train wagons, in the third class of a ship headed for the Amazon. The voyage of the rugged men (*arigós*) was hard. From Fortaleza to the rubber plantations, for example, could take up to three months. The only thing worse than the discomfort was the fear of sinking in the middle of the ocean. After all, in times of war, news of German U-boat attacks was not uncommon. In preventative efforts, the

Boat on River. *National Archives Building, Washington, DC (NAB)*

rubber soldiers received instructions and a life vest. In case of a shipwreck, in their pockets, there was a small provision of crackers and water. In the event, they were captured by the enemy, a cyanide pill. They had to choose between suicide and an enemy prison.

During the trip for the rubber soldiers, the only law was the "blackout law." Smoking or even lighting just one match was strictly prohibited. The ships that were full of rugged men were escorted by two mine-sweepers and a plane loaded with torpedoes. This was the safety strategy to prevent a German attack. Even a small light at sea would cause an uproar onboard. Sailors with binoculars on deck were carefully watching for a light on board or a sign of a possible enemy ship or submarine. There was fear among the passengers who didn't know how to swim. Beyond the fear was the poor treatment. The migrants were offered small quantities of terrible food. In many cases, entire families would wonder if there were even more dangers and difficulties to come.

The ship *Delaware* could haul up to two thousand passengers and two hundred tons of cargo, and was one of the fastest ships on the Amazon. *Delaware* operated between Belém and Manaus, where the trip took six days.

Boats at Dock. *National Archives Building, Washington, DC (NAB)*

The largest passenger transport and cargo ship was the Brazilian ship, *Lloyd*. There were also smaller transport ships that carried the *nordestinos*. And from the files of the US senate, there were pictures of converted war ships used in the exercise.

These smaller vessels, made in England, the US, and the Netherlands, took soldiers and merchandise to the rubber plantations up the rivers.

The larger boats with better accommodations—double-decker ships—were called *vaticanos*. The barges with a flat bottom were called *chatas*. Apart from these ships, the rugged men also traveled by launches, like the Higgins, manufactured in Brazil and financed by the American government.

Vintage US warships also transported the rubber soldiers one thousand seven hundred miles up the Amazon River, and brought the precious rubber balls back down the river to be transported to the US.

The tailor, João Rodrigues Amaro, now age seventy-two, left his girlfriend in Sobral, north of Ceará where he had a tailor shop and sewed a suit jacket per day to earn sixty *cruzeiros* (Brazilian currency of the time). The trip to "El Dorado" was certain to make him rich. The troops that left with him, climbed into the truck, singing farewell.

Warship at Sea. *National Archives Building, Washington, DC (NAB)*

From Maranhão to Pará, the boat trip made many people nauseous. On the ship Pedro I, where João Amaro embarked, there were more than one thousand two hundred northeasterners. Many soldiers took their families to the Amazon. But the tailor went alone, thinking about his white gold and his girlfriend who ended up getting married in his absence. In Belém, many of the troops waited twenty-two days for a steamboat that would carry them up river to the rubber plantations. A long wait for transportation was a sign of problems with available housing.

João Rodrigues Amaro. Araujo, Ariadne, *O Povo*, Fortaleza, Ceará, Brazil, Sunday, 21 June 1998

Upon landing in Maranhão, for example, the food was so bad, it

Workers Awaiting Ship. *National Archives Building, Washington, DC (NAB)*

caused a riot. Zé Doutor, a friend of João Amaro, was killed by a guard because he complained about the lunch. Around two thousand men rebelled and marched from Maracanã to São Luís in Maranhão. Almost an hour on the road, the army needed machine guns to calm the people down. The plan was to quickly put the entire group on a ship to Belém. But this wasn't always possible. What usually happened was they would spend long, unnerving days in port landings in the cities where they had to wait for transfers from one boat to another.[9]

The headquarters of some housing projects were much different than those made in Fortaleza. Barracks were built without partitions separating the sleeping areas, which were shared by men, women and children. João Amaro stayed in a landing where the communal bathroom was just a ditch, seven feet deep and seventy feet long. To use the improvised cesspit, a person would have to balance themselves on two planks stretching over the ditch. The rubber soldier tells us that due to the uncomfortable position and the risks required by the operation, once in a while, someone would fall in the hole. On these non-rare occasions, a rope would pull up the fallen person.

National Rubber Workers Awaiting Transport to New Tapping Sites in Belém, on July 27, 1943. *National Archives Building, Washington, DC (NAB)*

The rubber army arrived to the halfway point of the journey already on their last legs. The housing projects were surrounded and guarded by the military and when the rubber soldiers were allowed to wander freely through the towns, there were always difficulties with the local residents. According to João Amaro, the rubber soldiers from Rio de Janeiro were the fewest in numbers, but they caused the most problems. In the streets, they would forcibly kiss the girls and then start fights. The newspapers complained, "they are not the fine flour of the backlands, but the mud of the asphalt, the junk, robbing, killing, plundering, and wounding." Such was the reputation of the rubber army Getúlio Vargas had searched for in the Castinga forests of the northeast.[10]

One branch, the Amazon Navigational and Administrational Service of the Port of Pará (SNAPP or Serviço de Navegação da Amazônia e de Administração do Porto do Pará), had the responsibility of transporting the volunteer soldiers. The minister of the Economic Mobilization for the War Force, Lt. Col. João Alberto Lins de Barros did the math: the recruitment and transportation of men to the Amazon was about one hundred dollar a head. Beyond his calculations, he had a plan. To transport the troops, under strict military discipline, in a march to the strategic points, going town through Tocantins to the Amazon.

Pres. Douglas H. Adams, and Gov. Joachim Magalhaes Barata. *National Archives Building, Washington, DC (NAB)*

The plan was to construct forty checkpoints for room and board, and also inspections and medical assistance. The minister claimed to have crossed the entire area of six hundred miles on foot. The director of the Rubber Reserve Company (RRC), D. Allen called the proposition a bluff in poor taste. Critics argued that the route to Tocantins was overwhelming.

The plan was that the families of the volunteers would also be supported with food, schools and medical assistance. But, this did not hap-

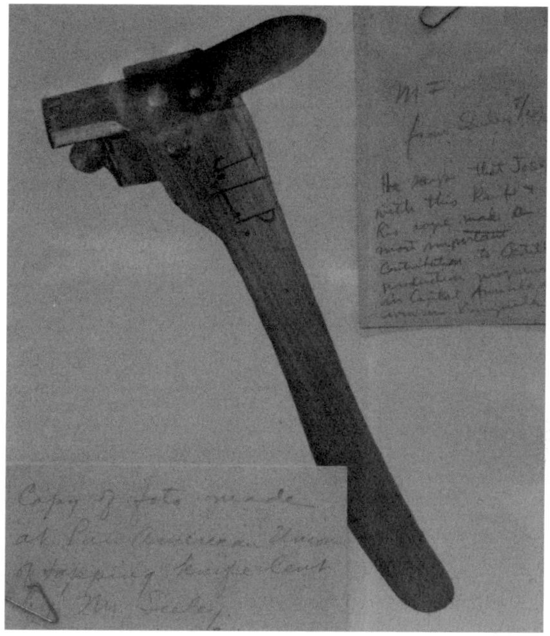

Rubber Tapping Instrument. *National Archives Building, Washington, DC (NAB)*

pen. The only matter of interest was the immediate transportation of men to the Amazon. A one way ticket where nothing that was promised counted anymore.

On his way back, after paying off his debt to the rubber plantation boss, in addition to his girlfriend, João Amaro found his mother had married as well. Two years in the Amazon rubber fields made João Amaro a skeleton suffering with malaria, yellow fever, and other jungle infections. His mother didn't recognize her own son: "I left chasing money, and came back poor and sick."[11]

As the northeastern recruits arrived at the rubber plantations, they were viewed with suspicion and mistrust. In the first place, they knew

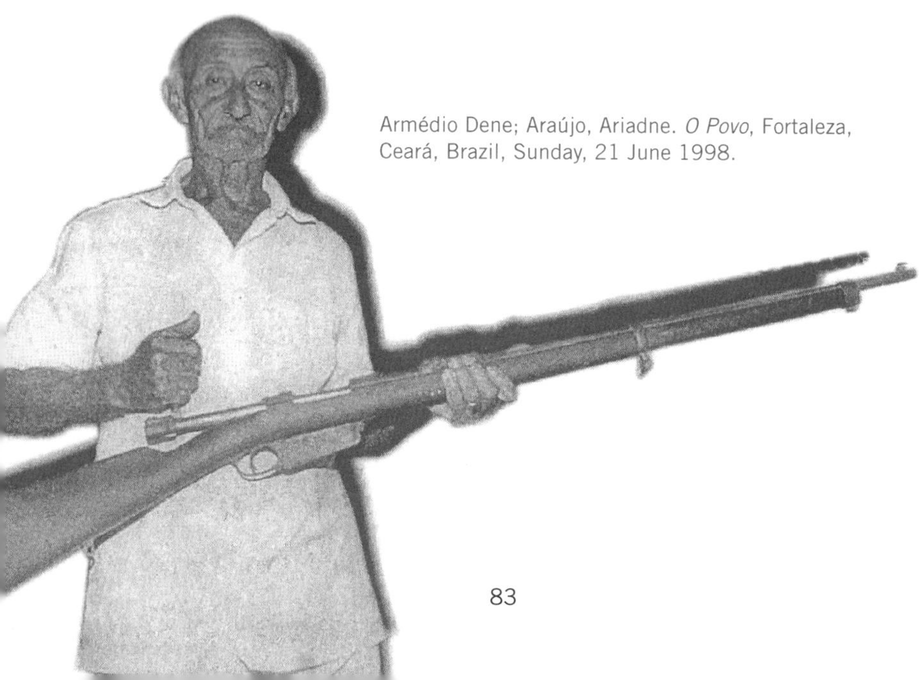

Armédio Dene; Araújo, Ariadne. *O Povo*, Fortaleza, Ceará, Brazil, Sunday, 21 June 1998.

nothing about the jungle and the technique of rubber tapping. One of the plantation bosses, Armedio, according to Ariadne: "They're all thieves and killers. They're all the same caliber as Lampião (the Jesse James of the Brazilian northeast). The only way to deal with a rugged man is with a rifle."

One of the main problems was that the northeasterners were famers and were forced to trade their hoe for the rubber tappers extracting knife. The climate in the Brazilian northeast was diametrically opposite to the climate in the Amazon basin and the northeasterners had little or no immunity to the fevers and illnesses of the tropics. Malaria, yellow fever, dysentery, and beriberi were merciless challenges for the northeastern rubber soldiers. Thousands of these rubber soldiers were sickened and died in the few years they labored in the Amazon forest. According to studies of the period, the soldiers who survived were those who married and lived with local Amazon women who were familiar with the ways of the people of the Amazon and the challenges of the jungle.

It was termed a debtors' prison. The soldiers arrived already in debt. A boss or a rubber tapper would record their debt, and they would work to pay it off. It was like unraveling a never-ending ball of yarn. There were always more debts to pay: food, clothing, guns, work supplies, medicine. Everything was sold to them at double the price. And the debt never seemed to go down, thus making the numbers seemingly endless. Invisible handcuffs for a deceived army. The northeasterners discovered exactly what the green hell was.[12]

CHAPTER 9

THE DAY-TO-DAY LIFE OF THE RUBBER SOLDIERS

In Ariadne Araújo's chronicle, she explains through various interviews with still living rubber soldiers in the Ceará region, their day-to-day trials. They left Ceará thinking that their experience would be much different than those of their fathers and grandfathers at the turn of the century when three hundred thousand nine hundred two people emigrated from Ceará from 1869 to the end of the century; two hundred twenty-five thousand five hundred twenty-six were destined for the Amazon. When the rubber boom ended in 1913, the majority of the survivors of this event returned to Ceará with little or nothing to show for their sacrifice.[1]

In the rush to provide the necessities for the rubber soldiers to begin producing rubber, one of the first major obstacles was the language problem. Very few of the Allied supervisors could speak Portuguese and very few of their Brazilian counterparts could speak or understand English. As a result, there was the "Case of the Missing Mules." In 1942, at least 1,581 mules were lost between São Paulo and Acre. The last word heard about these animals was after four months, when they hadn't arrived in Cuiabá. Another instance was when five thousand tons of flour was imported because of a mistake in the Portuguese to English translation. In this case, all the rubber soldiers wanted was some old cassava

Exercising at Pouso do Prado. *Foto Aba-Film: from the archives of the Universidade Federal do Ceará Museum of Art*

flour. The tailor João Rodrigues Amaro, now seventy-two (at the time of the interview in 1998), but at the time, seventeen, didn't find any of these mistakes made by the rubber campaign very funny.[2]

The elements were a constant challenge every day. There was incessant rain, mud, and clouds of pesky insects. Thousands of flies swarmed around the rubber soldiers wherever they went. There was an outbreak of meningitis in Belém as the soldiers waited for their transportation up river to the rubber fields; there was also a report of at least twelve deaths in the outbreak.

Even though the original agreements between the US and the Brazilian governments provided an upfront advance of five million dollars to improve sanitation conditions for the men, medical assistance was sparse and at best inadequate. A month with no deaths was celebrated. Routine medical exams, once promised, were rare and mostly limited to those with acute illness, and those with suspected sexually transmitted diseases.

Because of the large number of recruits, sometimes a thousand a day, transportation and housing became a critical issue, and sometimes hundreds of the soldiers would be stranded in ports along the river waiting to be moved on to the plantations. Because of the miserable circumstances, the men became unruly and difficult to manage. Ultimately, the Brazilian army had to step in and construct compounds surrounded by barbed wire to maintain order.

More Tires for Victory. *Chabloz: from the archives of the Universidade Federal do Ceará Museum of Art*

The men presented serious problems to the local communities along the river when they were allowed out of their compounds. There was a lot of drinking and fighting amongst themselves and the locals, which made life for everyone difficult. To the National Department of Immigration, these conflicts seemed like prison riots.

The agreements with the American Rubber Reserve Company made the responsibility of recruiting and transporting the rubber soldiers to their assigned rubber plantations entirely in the hands of the Brazilian government. From the very beginning, the US was concerned about the physical well-being of the rubber soldiers. Reports from US field inspectors about the health conditions of the rubber soldiers disturbed the Roosevelt government, and the president himself pushed the Brazilian government to improve conditions for the rubber soldiers. The Vargas Government actually emulated the Roosevelt government and setup multiple agencies to deal with these problems. One of these agencies that handled the recruitment and the housing projects was the Worker Mobilization Service in the Amazon called SEMTA (Service de Mobilização de Trabalhadores para a Amazônia). To complicate their near impossible task, many of the migrants came with their families and had children born during the voyage. With the US involvement, physical torture and abuse diminished in the 1940s.

The Vargas government endeavored to portray the responsibility of the rubber soldier similar to that of a Brazilian army regular and all of the government's propaganda was designed with that objective. The work field became the battlefield. Certain army terms like enlistment, recruitment, soldier, battle, and war were always present. In the national broadcast, the rubber program guaranteed the political involvement of its listeners. In the streets, the advantages of SEMTA were advocated in pamphlets. The propaganda said that the migrants were entitled to sixty percent of the rubber produced, fifty percent of the nuts harvested, fifty percent of the wood cut down, the right to hunt, fish, and keep the pelts of the slaughtered animals, and even a hectare (2.5 acres) of land to farm.[3]

Although the Vargas government had promised the rubber tappers sixty percent of the rubber they produced, the fact that they were obligated to sell all of their rubber to the estates and also buy all of their goods from the *aviadores*, almost negated this advantage. The prices they had to pay for necessities were elevated to keep the soldiers in debt. Another problem, which made it difficult to comply with the Vargas labor laws was the vastness of the region and the inability of the agencies to track the rubber tappers. Many of them moved from one estate to another, and some escaped to the cities to improve their quality-of-life. They wanted not only more comforts, but a primary education for their children.

In southern Brazil, Brazilian northeasterners have historically been looked down upon, with derogatory nicknames such as "*cabocolos,*" "*cabeça chata*" (flat heads), etc. A *cabocolo* is a mixture of a northeasterner and an Amazonian Indian, and the word *cabocolo* was used prominently in both the northeast and the Amazon, as well.

The recruitment campaign of the rubber soldiers was a national program, but due to the drought in the northeast and the great number of jobless men, the majority of the recruits came from the State of Ceará. With this in mind, the Vargas government propaganda machine convinced the thousands of recruits that life in a lush green forest, with good pay, good food and healthy conditions would be much preferred to that of their drought stricken northeast. It was an easy sell.

The Vargas Governments even convince the church officials in the region to participate in the campaign and priests were assigned to assist the families by SEMTA to provide counseling and religious assistance to the men and their families. SEMTA was for the single men, and CAETA

A rubber Tapper Leader Getting His SEMTA Arm Patch Identification. *Foto Aba-Film: from the archives of the Universidade Federal do Ceará Museum of Art*

facilitated some families to travel to an assigned rubber estate.

Rubber tappers accompanied by their families had better chances of survival on the rubber estates than those who lived alone, because their wives and older children could help sustain the family by growing mandioca and other crops, gathering fruits, and helping to smoke latex into large, coagulated balls. In late 1943, CAETA reversed SEMTA's policy on families and sent sixteen thousand two hundred thirty-five new rubber soldiers and eight thousand sixty-five dependents to the Amazon.[4] CAETA's decision reflected the government's longer-term goals of settling the Amazon with families of marginal rural poor from the Northeast. In contrast, SEMTA's policy of sending unaccompanied rubber soldiers was designed as a temporary measure to meet a wartime emergency.[5]

The SEMTA philosophy that the rubber business in the Amazon was mainly a man's business gradually changed, when it was determined that women could play an important role in gathering and producing rubber. As wives of the rubber tappers, they stabilized the family, but they were also involved in the production of rubber itself. Many women would tap the rubber trees at night, but were always in eminent danger. The fact that the Amazon was primarily a man's world, and women were in a huge minority, subjected them to all kinds of abuses—rape, assault, and the victims of brawling. They also had to contend with the rigors of the jungle, wild animals, brutal elements, and disease. Not only did women play an important role in the production of the rubber itself, but they were also skilled in working with the machines that dried and processed the latex.

Another agency created by the Vargas government was a special public health service, SESP (Serviço Especial de Saúde Pública), that established health posts on the main Amazon waterways and conducted campaigns to control the spread of malaria, yellow fever, dengue, etc.

Women Working with Rubber. *National Archives Building, Washington, DC (NAB)*

There was a plan setup for the men with families to have an amount of their salary deducted by the rubber estate and sent to the Rubber Credit Bank, which would send the money to the soldier's family in Ceará. However, this plan was never implemented as cash was never available because of the debit-credit system, and the rubber tappers' account was always in the red. The annual expenses of a rubber tapper were between four hundred dollar and five hundred dollar per year, while their income was only three hundred dollar. If rubber tappers were moved from one estate to another, their debts were transferred to the new estate of employment.

Not unlike Eva Peron in Argentina, Vargas liked to portray himself as the "Father of the Poor," but in reality, he paid little or no attention to the complaints and cries for assistance from the wives and children of the rubber soldiers. At one point, the Brazilian government canceled the financial assistance to the families. Using patriotic discourse, the women wrote that poverty had forced their men to go to the Amazon where they were serving their country by producing rubber for the victory of the United Nations. The telegram claimed that four thousand five hundred dependents of brave rubber soldiers serving on the Amazonian frontier would go hungry if President Vargas did not take action to reinstate their financial aid. The women lamented that they had not heard from their men since they departed, and did not know if they were dead or alive. The president's office referred the communication to CAETA, which rejected the complaint, declaring that the women acknowledged they had lived in misery even before their men left for the Amazon; therefore, CAETA did not consider itself responsible for their poverty.[6]

Consistent with its policy of allowing families to accompany rubber soldiers, CAETA offered the wives free transportation to the Amazon to join their husbands, but neither the families nor CAETA knew the locations of the rubber estates where their husbands and fathers worked. The government considered that its responsibility for the welfare of the rubber soldiers ended upon their arrival at the rubber estates. Its failure to keep track of the whereabouts of the rubber soldiers produced disastrous consequences, permanently separating workers from their families. To the destitute families left behind by the rubber soldiers, the "father of the poor" had become the "godfather of their poverty."[7]

Once the rubber soldiers were assigned to a rubber plantation they began their daily routine, which started in the middle of the night armed with a shotgun, a machete, a Jebond knife styled after the Asian rubber extraction knife, a kerosene headlamp, and a leather pouch with fuel. He would trudge the muddy paths of the forest seeking wild rubber trees, which were many times hundreds of yards apart; he would then slash the tree and attach the tin cup to gather the dripping latex. At the end of the day, he would retrace his steps and gather the latex that had accumulated. His machete cleared the jungle path, and his shotgun was his defense against wild animals, and possible Indian attacks.

Because of a labor shortage, the rubber bosses employed Indians to clear the trails for the rubber soldiers and some of them became efficient rubber tappers. The serangalists considered the Indians to be more dependable as they were better adapted and more self-sufficient than the rubber soldiers. The Indians had a better diet and enjoyed better health and were more resistant to disease. Even so, the Indians were only willing to work long enough to be able to purchase metal tools and other goods they could not produce themselves.

To the northeasterner the Amazon jungle could not have been a more opposite environment. Having been born and raised in a desert climate, he had difficulty adapting to the humidity and solitude of the jungle, and his immune system was not sufficient to ward off jungle diseases. But aside from all of these challenges, the most difficult was the absence of women in their lives. In fact, later studies indicated that the soldiers who

Volleyball at Pouso do Prado. *Foto Aba-Film: from the archives of the Universidade Federal do Ceará Museum of Art*

eventually married local Amazonian women were most likely to survive. In order to solve the problem, plantation bosses would bring in women from other places, but a common complaint among the workers was that the bosses themselves would take the best ones. Those that had wives always had the lingering fear that their wives would either be kidnapped or assaulted by either fellow rubber soldiers or Indians.

In an interview with rubber soldier Alcides Rodrigues Correa da Silva (seventy-eight years old in 1998), Ariadne Araújo quotes that he, "carried loads of latex on his back, about forty kilos in a basket made of vine, held by cords across the chest and forehead of the worker. On top of that, the route was eight hours per day, along the banks of the Juruá River in Cruzerio do Sul–Acre."[8]

In spite of the rigid work schedule, the rubber soldiers did find time for recreation. The plantation bosses would organize a weekend forró, which was a typical northeastern dance party for the single men. The party consisted of music and a lot of drinking of Brazilian *cachaça* (sugar cane rum). If there was no *cachaça* available, the men drank straight alcohol, and occasionally mixed the alcohol with milk, which they called "monkey tail." If there were no women to dance with, the men danced with men, but the party often ended in a brawl.

Even though the possibility of ever paying off their debts to the plantation owners was remote, they had a two-year contract and could not leave until their debt was paid. Occasionally, it would happen, and there were a few cases where the individual soldiers would liberate themselves from the rubber gathering and open small businesses along the river.

The mysteries of the Amazon have always fascinated outsiders, but these mysteries also fascinated and even terrified the Brazilian rubber tappers that came from their distant home in the northeastern State of Ceará. The Cearense, or Brazilian Nordestino, was as unfamiliar with the Amazon basin and its culture and challenges as the European explorers that visited the Amazon basin from the turn of the century.

As thousands of Cearense rubber tappers arrived in the Amazon basin to tap precious latex, from the turn of the century to World War II, the difficulty they faced in adapting, not only to a climate, which was totally different from their own, but also adapting to the myths and stories, which were perpetuated by thousands of rubber tappers who worked in the jungle over many years. These myths and legends have been passed on from one generation to the next and are even told today.

Many of these myths and legends have been recorded and published in a book by the Center of Workers of the Amazon (CTA, Centro dos Trabalhadores da Amazônia). *The Legend of the Mapinguari Devourer of Flesh, and Other Stories of the Rubber Plantations* was written by the actual rubber tappers, or rugged men (*arigós*). According to the authors, it's all true. In the book, the jaguar is one of the favorite myths. The jungle cat climbs up a tree and grabs an unsuspecting hunter, growls, and then goes for the dog. Francisco de Assis Monteiro tells of the day he went out to hunt with his son and managed to kill one. His accompanying dog was not as lucky. The dog took a claw to the face so hard that her head is now crooked.

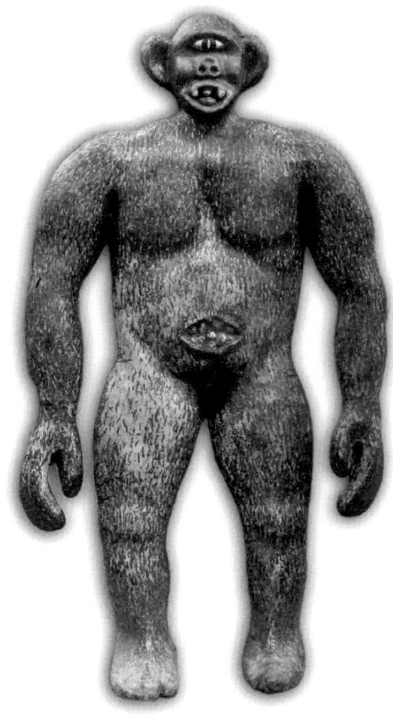

Mapinguari Statue in Parque Chico Mendes, in Rio Branco, Acre.

The *mapinguari* (a legendary enormous red sloth looking beast), the *curupira* (a mythical red headed, forest dwelling, demonic monkey), the Mother of the Forest, Matinta Pereira (a witch-like bird), *caboquinho* (another mischievous legend of the forest), all fascinated, cursed and tormented the rubber soldiers in the depths of the jungle. The myths of the Amazon were a part of the everyday life of the northeastern migrants.

The *mapinguari*, devourer of living flesh in the forest, was, according to the Apurinãs Indians: "six foot six, hairy, a thick hide, big sharp claws, one eye in the middle of his forehead and a huge navel that sprays a horrible odor that inebriates the hunter."[9] These myths terrified the rubber soldiers during late night latex extractions and even in recent years the inhabitants of the region are reminded of these stories and legends. Just one shot in the belly could kill the beast. In Chico Mendes Park, on the banks of the Rio Branco River in Acre, a life-sized replica of the *mapinguari* tells the story to visitors.

There are many dangers in the forest, both real and imagined, for those who come from the northeastern backlands. The *curupira* is red and takes on the form of a monkey with backward feet. If a hunter sees this creature, he won't be able to kill his prey that day. He gets really tired and unlucky. In order to trick the foolish hunter, the *curupira* can morph into a beautiful young girl and make the hunter get lost in the forest. If not for the *curupira*, then it might be the "Mother of the Forest" who punishes the rubber tappers for abusing the trees. She's old and skinny, but exacting and powerful. She whips dogs and can knock over a rugged man (*arigó*).[10]

Matinta pereira is a grey bird with yellow wings. Full of spells, sometimes she appears with a human face. *Caboquinho*, on the other hand, is a bit harder to be found because he's almost always invisible. He's short, gets around by foot, and has hair like a porcupine. *Caboquinho*, when bored, will whip a hunter with vines, leaving welts all over his body.[11] These were unwritten stories at the time that were told to recent arrivals at their parties.

Not all stories were myths and legends. There were true stories of life and death in the plantations, and Irlan Erasmo da Silva who heard this story from a rubber tapper in the Rubber Tappers Association told one such story to me.

José Costa was born in 1922, in Bahia in a place called Coração de Maria, in Feira de Santana. He came to the Amazon in 1943 as a migrant worker to work in a rubber plantations. Dona Raimunda Ferreira, the wife of rubber tapper/soldier José Costa, remembers this story. She's still alive, and lives in the city of Porto Velho:

> It was one of those suspicious days that José was working in the plantation shack in Triunfo, near the Bolivian border. He had stopped cutting rubber trees because the boss, Octavio dos Reis, found out that José could write a little bit and do some accounting. So, he went to work in the shed. From inside the shed, he overheard

two rubber supervisors chatting near the door. The two did not realize that José could hear what they were saying about Mario, a fellow tapper. They discussed what they were going to do with Mario, who was sick and wasn't doing anything. The two joked about the situation saying that a sick rubber tapper was like a dead tapir. The boss, in these cases, would usually kill the sick and throw the body in the river, then get another worker to replace him. It was like this in all rubber plantations, and the law should be fair to all. The other man agreed and said that they should put José in his place to cut the trees on Mario's route. The tapper, José Costa, soon realized that the two henchmen decided that Mario was going to die within two hours. Once the two became aware that José had overheard them, they threatened him, "Look Baiano (someone from Bahia), the saints don't know which Christian should die but we know when a Christian is dead and which one can stay quiet and alive."

José had learned from reading the capoeira stories in Bahia, and at this moment, he remembered a dream he had when he was a boy in which two sisters played happily in the forest and suddenly whistled just like a bird, "I am life, I am death." In front of the murderers, the tapper knew he was to remain silent without turning his back on the two. Everything on this Earth has its own timing according to the will of God, so also does man have his own will. And José decided Mário would not die, not in the hands of two miserable men of the devil.

He left the shed and secretly told Mario that the boss's henchmen were ready to throw his dead body in the river within a few hours. Mario, having learned of his death, didn't get out of his hammock, he was soaked in sweat from pain and fever. At that point, José knew he had to do something to save Mario's life, otherwise, it would be a sin. He decided to escape, even knowing that he would be carrying his friend on his back in the forest on a strange and unknown path and that the other men would be chasing him. Before fleeing, he returned to the shed and took all the ammunition that was there and threw it in the river. José was a step ahead of the men who would pursue him, and stayed away from the known "checkpoints" in the woods and margins of the river. When he left, he had a loaded shotgun and Mario on his back. It was the darkest part of the night; he had time to escape with just little or no hope of surviving.

After six hours of wandering through the black immenseness of the forest, tripping and getting all types of cuts on his body, the rubber tapper felt the weight of the world on his shoulders. He walked until daylight came through the forest and illuminated his mind. He masterfully cut off a few vines to fasten a jamachin (harness) that the rubber tappers and Indians used to lighten heavy loads, this time the load being a sick rubber tapper. He walked with the human burden on his back and the dedicated mission of not letting his friend, Mario die at the hands of men. Many hours passed, and after he made it another night, the rubber tapper collapsed with his jamachin harness. Mario, who was still alive, was able to say, "here on your shoulders, José, I'm seeing the last road of my life, and in the very same forest where my body will be buried, there will stand a cross."

The rubber tapper continued carrying his friend into the forest. In yet another dream, the same two sisters appeared to him, smiling as they did the time before and playing innocently under an enormous rubber tree. Life and Death say, "Thank God, José. There's someone who knows when you will die." But, José Costa didn't know and nothing could make him neglect his human burden over the space of thirty-three days in the forest. Eating berries, drinking water from vines, and rainwater. He didn't dream about the sisters ever again.

After thirty-three straight days by his friend's side, José saw a huge tapir[12] in a hole in the ground. Life had smiled upon them, and José killed it with his shotgun. On that day, Mario died, and José buried him in the same hole where he killed the animal to eat its liver. There he buried his friend and erected a cross.

Another story was told to our good friend, Irlan da Silva, an attorney for the rubber tappers:

> My name is Guiomar Ferreira. I was born on the banks of the River Madeira in the city of Humaitá in the state of Amazonas in 1928. I was named after my mother and my grandmother. I never knew my mother, as she died when I was born. I didn't know this until I was older when I was told that my first cry was the beginning of my life and end of my mother's life.

Chapter 9: The Day-to-Day Life of the Rubber Soldiers

I met my husband, Raimundo Lourenço in 1942, in Porto Velho, when I moved there after my father died. Shortly after I met him, he asked me to marry him. I was only fourteen years old and I didn't know much about life, but I did want to get married and didn't want to wait any longer. Three days after we were married, when I didn't know much about my husband, he said we were going to move to the border of Brazil and Bolivia so he could find a treasure. He said he had a dream that if he moved to the forest he would be able to find this treasure and he knew where he could find it. After he talked to me I started to cry, but I began to gather my things. My heart was so tight, it was like someone was stepping on my chest, but I was married to him, and even though I thought he was crazy, I knew I was married and marriage was just a onetime thing for me.

It was a time of war and Lourenço had just arrived from the northeast. He didn't know the difference between the Brazil nut tree and a rubber tree so he thought this was the treasure he was looking for. I also had my illusion because everyone thought they would be rich. I just didn't know how the milk from the rubber tree could make us rich. The trip to the area of the rubber tree near the Bolivian border was a like a war because everything was strange and new. Even the suffering of my young life did not prepare me for what I would be facing in the jungle. My husband didn't know anything either about the circumstances, and neither did his supervisor. Everything around us in the forest was strange and different and nothing consoled me. Every day was like it would never end. But gradually, I began to understand the value of my mysterious husband who would wake-up at every 0300 hours and take the path of the rubber tapper into the jungle and I would wait for his return with my heart in my hand until he arrived at about 1700 hours with a bucket of white gold from the rubber trees. We would than smoke the latex ball until 2000 hours and then prepare for the next day. He worked so hard and enjoyed his work and really didn't have any additional time to look for a treasure. Gradually, things became less strange and I learned that each day I had to learn something new like using the plants in the forest to make remedies and medicines to treat our ailments. My husband, who in the beginning did not know the difference between a Castaneda/Brazil nut tree, and a rubber tree, became an expert in collecting latex.

One day while crossing a river, my husband stepped on something and his foot bled like a river within the river. My world collapsed, as we had no medicine to help the awful pain he was suffering and it seemed only death would give him peace. He didn't die, but he could no longer stand or walk, and therefore could not work. I knew it was only a matter of time before his supervisor would know he was no longer of value. It was during this time that I heard him say the saddest words I have ever heard, "Guiomar you don't have to stay here with me. I can no longer work and therefore I cannot maintain a woman. Flee to the jungle camp and find your way out of here and leave me here to die in peace. Please obey me."

My life was never easy, but I never experienced pain like his words. I said, "I did not marry you to dishonor my parents by leaving the man God gave me. I will only leave here if you die. As of tomorrow I will take your place out cutting the latex trees, and you will wait for me to come with the latex and then you can help me smoke the latex ball. The supervisors will not know the difference. They will think you are doing the work and if sometime they discover I am doing the work, and they try to abuse me, I will protect myself with your shotgun. I don't have medicine to cure you, but I have faith and my faithfulness to you will make you well. I am now a rubber tapper." When he heard this he smiled.

Everything I said came true as if it was written and for a good amount of time, no one discovered that I was doing my husband's work in the forest. Then one day along the jungle path they found me with a bucket of latex in my hand, and almost dead of exhaustion. They said they had suspected something like this was happening because the amount of latex was diminishing. They said they did not have the right to have a woman doing this kind of work. With these words, they approached me, but they were looking down the barrel of my shot gun and with blood in my eye I spoke in a voice of such force that I did not know where it came from. The force of my resistance saved Lourenço's life and my life.

I went home and told Lourenco about my experience. He listened to everything very thoughtfully so that I hardly knew what to say. Six months had passed with Lourenço in the bed after that day when I told him about the men stopping me. After one year and ten months after the accident, Lourenço was able to get up

> again at 0300 hours and he left without saying a word. He returned at 1700 hours like he always had. He said the most beautiful words I had ever heard in all my life, "Guiomar, I am going again into the forest and for sure I have found my treasure. During the time I have been in the bed, every day that passed it was like my treasure was being polished. Today, when I was able to get up and go again into the forest I knew what is my treasure." I couldn't wait to ask Lourenco what is the treasure that you have been talking about. He smiled and said, "My treasure is inside my heart. God gave me the strength to cut the seringueira tree to sustain us, but He also gave me the knowledge necessary to recognize you, the treasure of my life. Your fidelity and your love, Guiomar is the best treasure any man could ever have and I can say for sure, I found my treasure the day I found you."

Of the thousands of migrant workers from Ceará who traveled to the Amazon for a better life, during the first rubber cycle at the turn of the century through the saga of the rubber soldiers during the war years, a relatively few ever returned home to Ceará. Many married Amazonian women and made their homes in the cities of Porto Velho, Rio Branco, Manaus and many other cities in the Amazon basin and thousands of them died of jungle fevers and other illnesses. In the city of Porto Velho, there is hardly a person among the four hundred thousand residents of today that does not have a relative among the original rubber soldiers.

During one of our trips to Porto Velho, we visited the refurbished Madeira Mamoré train station accompanied by members of the Association to Preserve the Madeira Mamoré River and Railroad. One of the group was a rubber tapper over ninety years of age and all of the other were descendants of rubber tappers.

The Brazilian word "*saudades,*" which is impossible to translate, but which all agree is a form of deep homesickness, was something that most all of the displaced Cearense had to content with. In order to ease the pain of being far from their homeland of Ceará, the rubber soldiers found comfort when the hamlets and villages in which they lived were named after the cities and town in their home state of Ceará, on the banks of the Juruá River in Acre, there's a rubber plantation called Fortaleza. But in the city of Cruzeiro do Sul, news is that there are dozens of places called Ceará, Rio Grande do Norte and Paraíba. Because of this, José Pereira da Silva (aged sixty-four in 1998) can say that he lives in "Fortaleza, the capital of where his father was born."[13]

Immigrant *Seringueiros* Arriving at Porto Velho. *National Archives Building, Washington, DC (NAB)*

The Author with Rubber Tapper and Rubber Tapper Descendants, 2010.

On the outskirts of Porto Velho, several hundred descendants of rubber soldiers live in poverty in a *favela* (slum), still waiting for the pension and profit sharing they were promised by the Vargas government in 1942.

The rubber tappers in the Amazon could be divided into two distinct generations. There were those that tapped rubber between 1850 and1912 during the first rubber boom, and who were known as the *flagelados*. In spite of the fact that their children and grandchildren followed them in the same industry, there was a great deal of difference between the two groups. The rubber soldiers, who tapped rubber during World War II, were an entirely different group of men. Although both groups of men migrated to the Amazon as a result of the drought and poor living conditions in the Brazilian northeast, they had entirely different motivations.

The early group went to the Amazon to improve their lives and search for fame and fortune. The rubber demand throughout the world attracted thousands of international speculators and fortune seekers, and the need for those who could extract the precious latex was in high demand. When the rubber boom died in 1913, a large number of the original *flagelados* made their way back to the northeast unhappy and disappointed with the experience. None of the things they had anticipated materialized.

Parade for the Rubber Soldiers with American and Brazilian Flags. *National Archives Building, Washington, DC (NAB)*

In contrast, the rubber tappers of World War II went to the Amazon with the conviction that they were contributing to an Allied victory and, as a result, they were buoyed up with a sense of patriotism and purpose. They left their hometowns throughout the northeast in high spirits, and even though, during the course of the war, they experienced many difficulties and hardships, not unlike their fathers and grandfathers, even today, they feel they made a significant contribution to the allied victory. Vargas, in his propaganda campaign, gave them pride, status, citizenship and lauded them as national heroes.

We are told by the legal representative of the Rubber Tappers Association in Porto Velho, Iran da Silva that past President Lula Inácio da Silva did provide the rubber tappers during his tenure, a partial pension. In 2010, the surviving descendants of the rubber tappers, now in their nineties and older, filed a suit against the Brazilian government to acquire additional compensation for the sacrifices of their fathers and grandfathers and themselves. The suit is still pending as of this writing.

Even in recent history, the rubber tappers have made international headlines. Chico Mendes, a third generation rubber tapper born in Acre, Brazil in 1944, would have arguably the most profound impact on the deforestation of the Amazon. He grew up on a rubber plantation, and

Chico Mendes. *Agência Brasil: Creative Commons Attribution 3.0 Brazil license*

by the age of nine, he already began to work as a rubber tapper. He had no access to schools and didn't learn to read until he was eighteen years old. In a revolutionary attempt to provide justice and protection to the workers and the forest, Chico Mendes helped found the Xapuri Rubber Tappers Union in 1970, and the much more influential National Council of Rubber Tappers in the 1985. Because of this, he faced fierce and sometimes violent opposition from the ranchers who exploited the tappers. Mendes's organizations served to provide safety for the workers and protection to the Amazon. Finding viable solutions to problems such as deforestation, road paving, and cattle ranching were at the center of his efforts.

In March 1987, Mendes was invited to Washington, DC, by the Environmental Defense Fund and National Wildlife Federation where he explained his ingenious idea of "extractive reserves" to the Inter-American Development Bank, World Bank, and US Congress. His idea of extractive reserves would take the land out of the hands of those who were profiting from its destruction and put it in the public domain. The land would then be used by the local population for subsistence farming of not only latex, but also oil, fruit, nuts, and other diverse riches the Amazon offers. His idea was a success, and today, extractive reserves account for more than eight million acres of the Amazon. At the time, despite his accolades, Mendes continued to receive constant death threats. One rancher in particular, Darly Alves Da Silva, seemed to want Chico Mendes dead more than anything.

In 1987, Darly purchased a plantation with intentions of exploiting it for rubber, but Mendes and his union resisted, eventually forcing Darly to step down. Towards the end of 1988, at the age of forty-four, Chico Mendes predicted that he would not live to see Christmas. This prophecy was fulfilled on 22 December, when Darly forcibly entered his home and shot him to death with a shotgun. Chico was just one of nineteen activists to be assassinated that year. Mendes's impact in his community, in the Amazon, and in the world, has transformed this humble rubber tapper into an icon, and his courageous martyrdom still inspires others to fight deforestation and oppression.

CHAPTER 10

RUBBER SHIPMENTS AND PAYMENT PROCEDURES

Although the United States (US) and Brazilian governments had come to a general understanding of their working relationship, there were still many issues that had to be resolved. Obviously, the US was anxious to move forward with rubber production, as they had less than one year of rubber stock in the country, but the Brazilian government also wanted to make sure that they were covered in all areas and they were not going to simply allow the US government a free hand. The Brazilians were also concerned about payment for the rubber, as was the US concerned about receiving the rubber upon payment.

As a result of these concerns on both sides, another series of communiqués were exchanged between the US Ambassador, Jefferson Caffery, in Rio, and the US Secretary of State, as well as with the Brazilian foreign office.

• • • • •

811.20 Defense (M) Brazil/328: Telegram
The Ambassador in Brazil (Caffery) to the Secretary of State[1]
Rio de Janeiro, 14 March 1942, 1600 Hours
[Received 1815 Hours]

871. For Rubber Reserves. Department's Number 640 on 13 March, 1900 hours. Will Firestone Tire and Rubber Company and Goodyear Tire and Rubber Company here continue to act as agents for Rubber Reserve under Agreement?

Please rush reply.

Caffery

• • • • •

811.20 Defense (M) Brazil/328: Telegram
The Acting Secretary of State to the Ambassador in Brazil (Caffery)[2]

Washington, 17 March 1942, 1500 hours . 671, Your 871 of 14 March. Firestone and Goodyear will not continue to act, as Rubber Reserve will deal directly with Bank of Brazil.

Welles

• • • • •

811.20 Defense (M) Brazil/335: Telegram
The Ambassador in Brazil (Caffery to Secretary of State[3]
Rio De Janeiro, 17 March 1943, 2100 Hours
(Received 2320 Hours)

918. For Rubber Reserve. Department's 640, 13 March 1900 hours. I have informed the Brazilian Government and the Bank of Brazil, Dr Truda of the Bank of Brazil[4] is of the opinion that the Government will expect Rubber Reserve to provide for the shipping arrangements.

Dr Truda says that the Government must promulgate a decree law establishing a single selling agency. He will discuss this and other matters with Souza Costa[5] who is returning today.

Dr Truda intends to establish buying offices at Belém and Manaus to purchase at the fixed price less a small discount for expenses of the selling agency, reselling only to established consumers within Brazil and to

Rubber Reserve. He will maintain a uniform selling price for domestic and export trade. He estimates domestic consumption at a maximum of ten thousand tons annually.

Dr Truda in complete agreement with the provisions of paragraph 3. He says that Brazil has recently exported 165 tons to Venezuela, 20 tons to Chile and that the Government will authorize shipment of 150 tons to Argentina, which were purchased several months ago, but he will not approve other requests.

He will adopt measures to prevent hoarding rubber by nonconsumers.

Caffery

• • • • •

811-20 Defense (M) Brazil/355
The Ambassador in Brazil (Caffery) to the Secretary of State[6]
No. 6764
Rio De Janeiro, 18 March 1942
(Received 23 March)

Sir, I have the honor to refer to the Department's telegram No. 623, of 12 March, 2100 hours[7] transmitting a note from Reconstruction Finance Corporation for the Bank of Brazil relative to the ten million dollars credit for the purchase of Brazilian rubber. The note was delivered to the bank of Brazil on 13 March 1942.

I enclose copies of the letter of acknowledgement of the Bank of Brazil and copies of the notice of registration of the credit.[8] The only difference between the note of the Reconstruction Finance Corporation and the credit registered by the Bank of Brazil is that the bank provides for three negotiable copies of the bill of lading, whereas the Reconstruction Finance Corporation calls for only two copies. Mr McAshan[9] perceives no objection to the procedure, provided the Bank of Brazil will forward the third negotiable bill of lading to the Federal Reserve Bank, when one of the first two negotiable bills of lading has been received in the US.

Please request the Rubber Reserve Company to confirm acceptance of the letter and enclosures of the Bank of Brazil.

The Bank of Brazil has suggested that original draft and documents referred to in the Department's telegram mentioned above be forwarded by air, second draft and documents by boat mail and third negotiable bill of lading to remain with the bank to be forwarded to the Federal Reserve Bank when one of the above originals has been received in the States. This suggestion is made to provide for the contingency if both remittances go astray.

Respectfully yours,

For the Ambassador;
JOHN F. SIMMONS
Counselor of Embassy

As mentioned earlier in the book, there has always been a lingering question in the minds of the representatives of the rubber soldiers in the areas of Acre and Rondônia about whether or not the US provided the agreed upon payments to the Brazilian government. The above document and exchange between the US ambassador Caffery and the US Secretary of State detailing how the payments were to be made, and to which organ of government, should erase any doubt that the agreed upon payments were made from the beginning and then subsequently as each load of rubber was shipped to the US. The mechanism of payment described in detail in the foregoing telegram would have made it impossible for rubber to leave the Amazon basin for the US without payment in hand.

• • • • •

811.20 Defense (M) Brazil/335: Telegram
The Acting Secretary of State to the Ambassador in Brazil (Caffery)[10]
Washington, 24 March 1942, 1800 Hours

749. Your 916 of 17 March. Proposal to Truda to permit export of one hundred fifty tons of rubber to Argentina would appear to violate terms of notes and rubber purchase agreements, as substances of these is that after date of signature Brazil will permit exportation of rubber only to this country. You are requested to point this out to Dr Truda and obtain his cooperation in preventing this shipment.

WELLES

In the foregoing telegram the US Acting Secretary of State Sumner Welles, protested Brazil's intention to fulfill Argentina's previous order of one hundred fifty tons of rubber reasoning that Argentina was an Axis collaborator, and that the requested rubber would be utilized for military purposes by the Axis powers. Italy had already established a Pirelli tire factory in Buenos Aires, and the US felt that this plant for manufacture of rubber tires would utilize this order of Brazilian rubber.

• • • • •

811.20 Defense (M) Brazil/361: Telegram
The Acting Secretary of State to the Ambassador in Brazil (Caffery)[11]
Washington, 27 March 1942, 2200 Hours.

799. Your 1008, 24 March, 1400 hours.[12] Suggestion that rubber Reserve station inspectors at Belém and Manaus to approve final quality and weights before shipment of rubber not practicable at present time.

Rubber Reserve agrees to amend letters of credit to permit single selling agency to draw for value rubber, less f.o.b. charges, in case export shipment not made within 30 days after the rubber available for shipment, provided rubber stored in public warehouses acceptable to Bank of Brazil and warehouse receipt delivered to American Consul at time of payment.

Rubber Reserve authorizes you to negotiate amendment to differentials contained Department's 640, 13 March within limits reported in Embassy telegram 689, 4 March,[13] but not over 19½ cents for crude Magabeira and crude Manioba or Ceará. Rubber Reserve recommends that differentials for both crude and washed Cameta also crude and washed Caucho be negotiated at or near the prices quoted for these grades in Department's 640, 13 March.

Reply will be made at a later date to suggestions connection Article 7 agreement.

WELLES

In the exchange of messages between Brazil and US, there was great concern that the other American republics would not be able to receive enough manufactured tires for their needs, and Brazil and US were desperately trying to find a solution to this growing problem.

• • • • •

811.20 Defense (M) Brazil/ 525: Telegram
The Ambassador in Brazil (Caffery) to Secretary of State[14]
Rio de Janeiro, 1 May 1942, 1800 Hours
(Received 2252 Hours)

1486. For Finletter,[15] Newhall Clayton,[16] Klossner,[17] from Allen.[18]

Department's 1076, 24 [25] April, 0000 Hours, and my 1443, 28 April, 2100 Hours.[19]

Following agreement reached at meeting with Brazilian rubber manufacturers and members Brazilian Commission subject approval Finance Minister.

1. Annual over-all quota ten thousand tons dry weight rubber and reclaim.

2. Minimum of twenty-five percent of quota to be devoted to manufacture essential products for export to apply against essential Western Hemisphere requirements as determined by Washington thereby in effect establishing maximum internal quota of 7,.500 tons.

3. Rubber Reserve to purchase exportable surplus tires and tubes at equivalent of net Rio de Janeiro dealer prices as approved by Brazilian Government.

4. Export of tires and tubes to countries other than US prohibited effective immediately regardless of licenses outstanding. Necessary instructions already issued by Finance Minister.

5. Manufacturer's miscellaneous rubber goods willing discontinue manufacture nonessentials and restrict exports to the US provided prices agreed upon and orders placed for tires and other essential rubber products. Advisable US give earliest possible assurance these countries with respect supply essential requirements.

Roberts[20] remaining Rio de Janeiro until end next week to conclude negotiations miscellaneous products will then join us Lima. Urgently need information requested our telegram 1225, 10 April,[21] midnight. About miscellaneous rubber products for meeting with manufacturers 7 May. Telegraph basic information if cannot be airmailed.

Official price schedules have been published in Brazil thereby facilitating resumption shipment.

Believe proportion exportable surplus may run higher than twenty-five percent because of acute storage gasoline and drastic gasoline rationing which already has materially reduce nonessential driving and demand for tires.

Strong diplomatic pressure being brought to bear upon Brazil by other Latin American countries to supply essential export products.

6. All manufacturers willing use approximately same proportion reclaim as now used in US when available.

7. Brazil desires develop maximum possible domestic supply reclaim and requests US facilitate shipment pan reclaim equipment.

Telegraph if pan reclaim can be satisfactorily used in same proportion as digested reclaim in United States of America (USA).

8. Brazilian Commission is recommending 2-year suspension of duties and other obstacles to importation and use of reclaim from the US. Brazil willing use reclaims from the US to extent their domestic supply inadequate to comply with paragraph 6.

9. Brazil to undertake campaign to bring about economy in use of rubber products.

10. United States to facilitate shipment materials needed by rubber manufacturing industry with respect to which Brazil is dependent from US.

11. United States to give assurance to Brazil with respect to supply rubber goods essential for Brazilian military and industrial purposes or equipment for manufacture thereof. (Allan)

Caffery

The foregoing memorandum of understanding precisely detailed the rubber policy between US and Brazil going forward. It should be noted that all of these negotiations took place in the brief period between the attack on Pearl Harbor on 7 December 1941, and the end of May 1942.

In early 1944, a special commission formed to study the supply and stocks of war material, was the one to sound the alarm. In 1944, about twenty-seven million automobiles in the US were abandoned due to a lack of tires. Cars aside, the production of other items was affected, such as footwear, insulation, belts, and radio and telephone parts. The stored supply would only last another twelve months, at the most. The military planners were in a panic. But, the weapons industry was given priority. Better discomfort than defeat.

The commission's final report left no doubts. If new supplies were not secured, the needs of the military would use up everything in stock—six hundred forty-one thousand tons before the summer. The path would be one of sacrifice. At first, for the American civilians, and soon after for thousands of Northeastern Brazilians. In order to reduce the consumption of tires, the US rationed gasoline, implemented thirty five miles per hour speed limits, limited the yearly mileage of a car to five thousand miles, and even suspended the production and sales of automobiles until further notice.[22]

• • • • •

811.20 Defense (M) Brazil 516: Telegram
The Secretary of State to the Ambassador in Brazil (Caffery)[23]
Washington, 6 May 1942, 2200 Hours

1164. Your 1442 of 28 April and 1486 of 1 May. For Donnelly and Allen, all here concur in feeling that you have obtained excellent results in your negotiations with respect to internal consumption and manufactured products.

The agreement outlined in your 486 of 1 May is in general satisfactory.

Under points 2 and 3, it is understood that Rubber Reserve purchases the exportable surplus of tires and tubes and then uses them in supplying essential Latin American requirements.

The wording of point 5 is not as clear as it refers to the advisability that the US give earliest possible assurance to "these countries" with respect to the supply of essential requirements. It is assumed that you refer to other Latin American essential requirements for miscellaneous rubber goods. In the agreement with Peru, this Government agreed to collaborate with Peru in the view of assuring to Peru an equitable distribution of supplies of rubber products available to US and Peru on the basis of relative needs and of the present emergency. It is probable that similar assurances will be given to the other countries, which have broken with the Axis.

Following is estimated use of miscellaneous rubber products in long tons of crude rubber content during 1940: Argentina 145; Bolivia 30; Chile 195; Colombia 126; Ecuador 21; Panama 36; Paraguay 3; Peru 58;

Uruguay 29 and Venezuela 147.

Following is estimated use of 1942 requirements for essential needs of miscellaneous rubber products in long ton of crude rubber content: Argentina 50; Bolivia 38; Chile 158; Colombia 76; Ecuador 6; Panama 12; Paraguay 6; Peru 59; Uruguay 27 and Venezuela 82. No breakdown of products is available at present time.

The estimate of Argentina's requirements is recognized as low, but it is felt that with strict limitation in Argentina there is sufficient rubber in stock to care for requirements for rest of year, except for a small allocation to cover special types of products.

These figures represent only present intentions here and it should not be implied that this country is to be bound to supply such amounts to these other countries.

The answer to question under point 7 depends on the product for which the reclaim is to be used. Goodyear and Firestone have been asked to furnish additional information on this question and it will be transmitted on receipt.

With respect to points 9 and 10, the US will agree to do everything possible to facilitate these shipments so far as consistent with the relative emergency needs of the two countries.

HULL

• • • • •

811.20 Defense (M) Brazil/ 780: Telegram
The Ambassador in Brazil (Caffery) to Secretary of State[24]
Rio de Janeiro, 13 May 1942, 1500 Hours

[Received 1830 Hours]

1615 For Finletter, Clayton, Newhall, Klossner.

Mr Boucas[25] informs us that he understood the five million dollars fund referred to in clause 4 of the rubber agreement of 3 March[26] and in numbered paragraph 1 of Souza Costa's note to Mr Welles dated 3 March[27] was to be in addition to the quantity premium payable on rubber in excess of five thousand and ten thousand tons annually. Mr Boucas stated that his understanding reached in Washington was that the premiums would be paid over to the Instituto Agronômico do Norte or the new rubber Institute and not used as a credit against the five million dollars fund.

We had understood that the premiums as due would be credited against any part of the five million dollars fund which had been used in Brazil for the purpose of increasing rubber production until that part of the five million dollars fund so used had been covered after which any such premium would then be paid outright to the appropriate Brazilian government agency.

In order to avoid serious misunderstanding at this end, it is urgently requested that you telegraph your interpretation as soon as possible.

CAFFERY

• • • • •

811.20 Defense (M) Brazil/606: Telegram
The Ambassador in Brazil (Caffery) to Secretary of State[28]Rio de Janeiro, 19 May 1942, 1600 Hours
(Received 20 May, 0103 Hours)

1696. Department's 1245, 16 May, 1400 hours.[29] The Minister of Finance on 28 April (see my 1442, 28 April, 2100 hours)[30] instructed the Director of the Export-Import Department of Bank of Brazil to prohibit the exportation of crude rubber in any form and tires and tubes except to the US. The Minister of Finance confirmed the instruction in writing last week and he again instructed the Bank of Brazil to cancel all applications for the exportation of these products.

With regard to the letter from the American Embassy in Buenos Aires the shipments referred to were made under licenses obtained prior to the agreement of 3 March between Brazil and US. The other cases referred to in the Department's telegram are covered by prohibition cited in the first paragraph.

CAFFERY

811.20 Defense (M) Brazil 538: Telegram
The Secretary of State to the Ambassador in Brazil (Caffery)[31]

Washington, 21 May 1942, 1700 Hours

1301. In further reply for your 1576, 9 May[32] Rubber Reserve is prepared to purchase all miscellaneous rubber items already manufactured and in process and all future items made available during the life of the Agreement of 3 March at net dealer prices now prevailing in Brazil, subject to change by mutual agreement.

In so far as practicable Agreement should provide for purchase of essential items, the production of which is permitted under the terms of west palm beach (WPB) permissive order M-15-b, as amended.

The agreement with Rubber Reserve should provide that Rubber Reserve Company is entitled to change the items on the list and specifications therefore with due protection to the interests of the manufacturer. Rubber Reserve will make necessary arrangements to finance the acquisition of these items and their storage in Brazil. It is understood that this offer applies only to those manufactured goods produced within the quota fixed by agreement for Brazil's domestic industrial consumption of crude and reclaimed rubber.

The agreement is not limited to the acquisition of essential products. This is for two reasons. In the first place, we do not have here detailed information as to Brazilian production facilities for miscellaneous products and hence cannot determine to what extent it would be feasible to manufacture items regarded here as essential. Second, we do not have detailed information as to the requirements of the other Latin American Republics for miscellaneous products. For these reasons, Rubber Reserve Company is planning to send to Brazil in the very near future a representative familiar with conservation policies here who will aid in changing over to the manufacture of essential items, and we can proceed with the obtaining of the necessary information for the other Latin American Republics. In the meantime, however, Rubber Reserve Company desires to acquire all manufactured products not required for domestic consumption in Brazil.

Repear to Lima for Allen as No. 43.

HULL

The rapid-fire exchanges between Brazil and US regarding rubber quotas for the other Latin American Republics, underscored the urgency of finding a solution to the problem of fulfilling the needs of the other republics. The US made clear that they would be willing to take into consideration the requirements of those republics that had separated themselves from the Axis powers, but they also made clear that the Rubber Reserve Company of the US would make the final decision as to the quotas for each country.

• • • • •

811.20 Defense (M) Brazil/721a: Telegram
The Secretary of State to the Ambassador in Brazil (Caffery)[33]
Washington, 13 June 1942, 1800 Hours

1532. Your 1804 28 May.[34] The general purpose of the development fund of five million dollars is to make available in Brazil funds for taking all action necessary to increase the production of raw rubber as fast as possible. Implied in this general purpose, however, is the limitation that the fund is not to be used unless, and only to the extent, it is needed for this purpose.

The fund is primarily available for subsidies without obligation of repayment. Included in such subsidies, per the terms of paragraph 4 of the agreement of 3 March 1942, are premiums for raw rubber purchased by the Rubber Reserve Company. These premiums are to be credited against the fund and turned over to the Brazilian Government to be expended by that Government for raw rubber development projects.

Where a request is made for a subsidy from the fund the governing consideration should be the importance of the project for which the subsidy is requested to expeditious production of raw rubber. Subject to this consideration, however, the following may also be taken into account: (1) Whether the project is commercially feasible on a profit basis without subsidy or with only partial subsidy; (2) If it is, whether there is assurance that it will be undertaken at the earliest possible moment regardless of a subsidy.

The fund is also available for loans. As in the case of subsidies, the governing consideration in passing upon a request for a loan is the importance of the project for which the loan is sought to expeditious production of raw rubber. Subject to this consideration, however, the following may also be taken into account: (1) Whether the project is such as is financed by loans according to the usual practice of the industry; (2)

Whether the project is a sound risk according to ordinary standards of banking practice and (3) If it is a sound risk whether there is assurance that it will be financed by private sources of capital at the earliest possible moment. The amount of loans granted should be deducted from the fund in the same manner as subsidies in order to determine the balance on hand at any particular given time; but moneys received in repayment of the principal of such loans immediately should be returned to the fund and become available for re-expenditure.

It is suggested that in so far as possible requests for loans to finance projects, which are commercially sound be granted from special funds to be setup by the Rubber Reserve Company. This would prevent undue depletion of the of the five million dollars fund, which may be used to finance any project necessary to expedite raw rubber production regardless of how bad a commercial risk the project may be.

In accordance with what has been said previously with respect to granting subsidies from funds, and for more specific guidance with respect to the same, the following are suggested as illustrative of projects meritorious of subsidy: This list is merely illustrative and is by no means to be considered exhaustive.

The improvement of transportation and communication facilities, such as acquisition of vessels, building of roads into remote rubber producing areas (e.g., those in Mato Grosso), construction of airfields, and provisions of short-wave radio transmitters to agents at key points within the Amazon basin.

The preparation of facilities for tappers, moving into production areas is likewise a primary expenditure to be met from the fund. This would include the building of houses and barracks, construction of supply and medicine depots (including launch dispensaries), movement of foods and medicines into the selected areas, and organization of subsistence agriculture (including provision of seeds and implements) in so far as necessary to assure food supplies and minimize import requirements from outside the Amazon system.

Distribution by public authority of foods, tools, medicines and supplies for tappers controlled so far as necessary to assure that they reach the tappers.

As the program expands large-scale immigration into the Amazon may become essential. It is contemplated that this will involve large-scale preparations in advance of settlement and possibly subsidization of transport into the area and of operations there during a preliminary period.

In as much as the fund is setup to provide for direct developmental costs, salaries and general administrative overhead of Rubber Reserve officers in Brazil shall not under any circumstances be met from the fund.

With respect to arrangements heretofore proposed, on the basis of the foregoing the following treatment would be accorded. The supplies referred to in his 1484 of 1 May[35] appear to be commercially profitable and a financing problem is involved. The five hundred million dollars fund made available for that purpose will accordingly been restored to the fund to the extent repaid. On the other hand, the credit of fifty thousand dollars, opened to build barracks and pay transportation does not appear to be a commercial undertaking and hence would be paid for out of the fund and reduce the amount thereafter to be available. The five hundred million dollars made available for special loans pursuant to Department's 1269 of 18 May would be on the same basis as the five hundred million dollars made available for financing the purchase of supplies. The expenditures of fifty thousand dollars, each for projects approved by McAshan in Department's 1365 of 27 May[36] would also presumably not be a commercial proposition and hence paid for outright and finally from the fund.

Please advise whether you and McAshan concur in the foregoing.

HULL

CHAPTER 11

BANKING CHANGES

To finance this ambitious enterprise to increase rubber production, the Brazilian government created the Banco de Crédito da Borracha (BCB) through Decree-law 4.451, on 9 July 1942. The Rubber Credit Bank, with its headquarters in Belém, had the exclusive right to buy and sell crude rubber, both for export and to supply Brazil's[1] manufacturing industry. The Brazilian government capitalized the bank by buying fifty-five percent of its shares. The United States (US) government, through the Rubber Reserve Company, bought forty percent, and the remaining five percent of shares were made available to private Brazilian investors. The total initial capital invested was fifty thousand Brazilian *contos*, or two million five hundred thousand dollars.[2] The bank presidency was reserved for a Brazilian citizen, and the board of directors was composed of two North Americans and three Brazilians.

The purpose of the Rubber Credit Bank was to make loans to rubber producers as well as to individuals and companies involved in extraction, trade and industrialization of rubber. The bank was authorized to provide financial assistance for: supplying rubber estates; developing transportation between production centers and the market places of Belém and Manaus; preparing and colonizing the most productive zones for planting and cultivating the best rubber trees identified by the Brazilian Agronomic Institute of the North; and organizing cooperatives of rubber tappers and small producers.[3]

Banco de Crédito da Borracha. *National Archives Building, Washington, DC (NAB)*

• • • • •

811.20 Defense (MJ) Brazil/820: Telegram
The Ambassador in Brazil (Caffery) to Secretary of State[4]
Rio de Janeiro, 10 July 1942, 2000 Hours
(Received 2127 Hours)

2480. For Finletter and Allen. Rubber Reserve. Presidential decree of law of 9 July, created Banco de Crédito da Borracha with capital of fifty thousand contos (Brazilian Currency) of which Brazilian Government will subscribe fifty-five percent, Rubber Reserve forty percent and Brazilian public five percent. The three directors will consist of two Brazilians and one American. Brazilian Government has approved appointment E.E. Longas, American director, but has not yet named its directors, one of which will be president of bank.

Proportionate stock ownership was changed without our knowledge from the original agreement of fifty to fifty participation. Boucas explains that new setup is necessary under corporation law requirements of Brazil. Brazilian authorities have assured us that no loans, commitments or undertakings will be concluded without written approval of American director. This is the first time under existing banking legislation that Brazil has permitted foreign stockholders and director and as such represents important concession to the US and is so interpreted here.

If we had been consulted in advance, we would have approved the change in proportionate stock ownerships. We regard the decrees and statutes of the bank as satisfactory and feel that the measure will greatly facilitate financing of entire rubber program. (Text by airmail)

CAFFERY

The importance of the foregoing communiqué in which it is announced that Vargas decreed a major change in Brazilian banking laws demonstrates the critical importance of the whole rubber project. As both governments scrambled to devise a structure under which the US could transfer critically needed funds to the rubber gathering project in the Amazon, both countries came to an accommodation so that the bank transfers could begin immediately. Even though the US under Brazilian law, could not be an equal partner in the banking structure created, it was made clear that the US had veto power in any questionable transaction.

The Rubber Credit Bank was a direct challenge to the interests of the great Amazonian trading houses, which had made fortunes from trading over-priced supplies and imported food to the rubber estates on credit in exchange for future deliveries of crude rubber and other primary forest products. Trading posts on rubber estates over-charged for vital supplies and foodstuffs and paid artificially low prices for the crude rubber production of the tappers. Rubber tappers were not paid in cash; instead, they had running accounts with their estates' trading posts, which they were obligated to settle before they were permitted to leave.[5]

• • • • •

811.20 Defense (M) Brazil 935: Telegram
The Charge in Brazil (Simmons) to the Secretary of State[6]
Rio de Janeiro, 1 August 1942, 2000 Hours
(Received 2 August, 0327 Hours)

2832. For Clayton, Finletter, Hays,[7] Bicknell[8] from Allen, McAshan, Micou.[9] Confirming telephone conversation of today with Cooke,[10] Brazil has requested that tires and tubes for shipment from Brazil to American countries other than the US be not purchased by Rubber Reserve but be sold and shipped by Brazil to such countries under an agreement between Brazil and Rubber Reserve whereby Brazil would agree that shipments of tires and tubes from Brazil to each such country would not exceed the quota established by the US for the essential needs of each such country.

The reason for this request by Brazil is that Brazil desires to retain its normal trade relations with the countries concerned and does not wish to appear to have such trade under direct control of the US. In this connection, the Brazilian Foreign Office has sent a strong note to the Embassy expressing this point of view and taking the position that the rubber agreement between Brazil and US only contemplated that Brazil would sell the US its exportable surplus of crude and manufactured rubber to fill the needs of the US but not for redistribution by the US to other American countries. Brazilian Government feels so strongly on this matter that they withheld export permits covering shipment of tires to Peru now in process of loading, but we were able to have them agree to issue the licenses upon the understanding that this whole question would be explored with a view to considering an adjustment of the present arrangements for the purchase of tires and tubes in Brazil by Rubber Reserve for distribution to other American countries.

The agreement with Brazil limiting consumption of crude rubber within Brazil and the relating agreement to purchase tires and tubes is set forth in Allen's letter to Boucas originally dated 27 April 1942, later slightly changed and redated 2 May.[11] This letter must be read in conjunction with memorandum presented to Brazilian Commission 28 April 1942, setting forth the principles agreed upon. Both of these documents are attached to Allen's report number 3, item number 8.[12] The agreements referred to have been reorganized by Brazil in practice, but have not been officially confirmed. Brazil has not yet taken the position that the agreement is not in effect. It must be remembered, however, that the agreement for limitation of consumption of crude rubber within Brazil was wholly voluntary act of cooperation by Brazil and was agreed to by Brazil despite the specific provisions of the rubber agreement between Brazil and US, which contemplated the expansion of rubber manufacture in Brazil. In view of this situation, it is important that the US avoid any appearance of dictation or arbitrary control and as long as Brazil specifically agrees to keep its sales and shipments of tires and tubes to other American countries within the quotas established by the US, the main purpose of the US is accomplished. Furthermore, the request of Brazil is in our opinion, in accord with the understanding set forth in the memorandum of principles agreed upon by Rubber Reserve and Brazil, which was the foundation for the agreement set forth in Allen's letter to Boucas.

If the request of the Brazilian authorities is granted, it should be made clear that it is without prejudice to our rights under paragraph 7 of the main Rubber Agreement of 3 March.[13]

In any case, we will attempt to negotiate early next week an agreement permitting Brazilian manufacturers and exporters to buy and ship from Rubber Reserve present stocks in Brazil in order to liquidate our stocks first before new production is exported. We will also endeavor to arrange for the continuance of the system whereby we purchase all tires and resell to foreign or Brazilian buyers for exportation since Mr Cooke has informed us that Brazil's production is approximately equivalent to total requirements of other Western Hemisphere Republics. To facilitate these discussions please cable third quarter allocations each Western Hemisphere Republic so far arranged and prospects arranging allocations any other.

If we are unable to make these arrangements suggested by Cooke then we recommend granting Brazil's request outlined in early part of this cable and subject to the conditions set forth, otherwise we fear the breakdown of the entire consumption agreement. (Allen, McAshan, Micou)

SIMMONS

Notwithstanding the many exchanges between the two governments in a quest to find common understanding on how the Brazilian rubber was to be distributed, there was still a very serious unresolved issue. The Brazilians thought they had the upper hand as in the final analysis; they controlled the rubber production, and when they insisted, the Brazilian producers sell rubber products directly to the other American republics, the US took issue. The concession by the Brazilians was that they would not exceed the quotas, which had been determined by the US for each of the other republics involved, but the US Secretary of State (Hull) came back in the following memorandum with other serious concerns. The memorandum provides careful detail of what Secretary Hull felt had to be the basis of the final agreement. As far as the Brazilians were concerned the reason for their insistence on maintaining control of the delivery of rubber products to the other republics was that they did not want to appear to be under the control of the US government, but Hull in his memorandum addresses this issue as well by suggesting that the US and Brazil jointly accept the orders from the other Republics to be filled either directly from Brazil or the US.

• • • • •

811.20 Defense (M) Brazil/959: Telegram
Secretary of State to the Ambassador in Brazil (Caffery)[14]
Washington, 12 August 1942, 2200 Hours

2251. Your dispatch 8073, 31 July,[15] and Telegrams 2832, 1 August and 2855, 3 August.[16] There are certain distinct and important advantages, which the present arrangements on Brazilian manufactured products afford to Brazil. In the first place, Brazil is assured a market for these products for the terms of the contract at a price fixed by Brazil. Under the arrangements, now in effect Rubber Reserve has purchased almost three million dollars' worth of Brazilian tires. Rubber Reserve pays cash immediately. The manufacturer does not have to wait for shipping to be available before getting his money. Rubber Reserve buys the tires and puts them in a warehouse and pays the warehouse charges, an arrangement, which permits normal operations by the manufacturers unaffected by shipping situation. The manufacturers in turn are able to keep their workers steadily employed. They are assured a guaranteed market for 5 years, at a time when Brazil's consumption of tires has been tremendously reduced and then demand in other countries cannot be considered assured. It seems to us unlikely that Brazil could obtain similar undertakings from other sources.

It should also be kept in mind that this Government is supplying to the manufacturers various materials required in tire manufacture, such as bead wire, which Brazil cannot obtain elsewhere. This government is also giving sympathetic consideration to the application by the Goodyear Company of Brazil to export machinery for manufacturing rubber belting.

Acting in reliance on the arrangements worked out by Allen, and compiled with in practice by Brazilian authorities, Rubber Reserve has made commitments to furnish tires in specific amount to Colombia, Peru and others. This Government also gave undertakings to all other American Republics to supply their indispensable requirements for tires. See the Department's circular telegram of 18 May.[17] These undertakings were entered into at the urgent request of the Brazilian Government, and it was assumed the exportable surplus of Brazilian tires would be available to fill them. Even if the understanding set forth in Allen's letter of 2 May[18] was not formally acknowledged, there can be no ambiguity about the meaning of paragraph 7 of the 3 March agreement, which Boucas advised had been cleared by telephone with President Vargas. Moreover, the second paragraph of Allen's memorandum handed to Souza Costa, Boucas and Truda on 28 April[19] leaves no doubt as to the intentions and understanding of this Government in making the arrangements proposed to Brazil.

Aside from the advantages of the present system to Brazil and without regard to its contractual status, the following considerations appear to us to make the abandonment of the present system inadvisable.

1. This Government has no desire to limit or interfere with Brazil's trade relations with the other American Republics, or to obtain control of any of those relations as such.

2. There is a limited and small amount of rubber products available for the indispensable needs of the American Republics. It is urgently necessary that the distribution of available supplies should be made equitably and based upon the essential wartime requirements of the countries.

3. The Brazilian Government will appreciate that an equitable distribution can be attained only through the exercise of adequate controls. A particular purchaser should not get the disproportionate number of tires. Information as to the sizes and types must be considered in each case to determine whether the order is justified. Sales should not be able to be made to undesirable purchasers. Shipments should be arranged so as to coordinate available shipping space with consumption needs. Supplies should be integrated so as to make a pool available to meet orders for various sizes and types. Otherwise there will be inefficiency in filling orders. Rubber Reserve is prepared to create that pool and maintain balanced inventories.

4. It has taken this government two years to establish adequate controls for exports from this country. Operations under the control machinery is understood and accepted by the various importing countries.

5. The establishment of quotas for exports from Brazil without further implementation is not sufficient. It is extremely doubtful whether Brazil would strictly uphold the quota system under the stress of diplomatic or internal political pressure. In any event, certain requirements for tires and other products must be furnished from this country (including in the case of Brazil, tires for airplanes and other equipment for the Brazilian armed forces) because they cannot be manufactured in Brazil.

Information as to shipments from Brazil and the US must be coordinated so as to be available in passing on any particular shipment from either country.

6. The contract now being negotiated with Mexico[20] contemplates that Mexico will sell to the US its exportable surplus of manufactured products. Venezuela might conceivably become an exporter of tires. It is therefore quite clear that some single entity must administer the distribution of tires available for export from this country, Brazil, Mexico and any other exporting country.

7. A control system might be established in the Embassy, but this would result in duplication of personnel and almost endless checking back and forth between the Embassy and the agencies here.

8. As a theoretical matter, the administrative entity might best be an inter-American commission. It appears to us hopeless to expect that such a commission could function efficiently at any time in the near future. This government is prepared to consider the establishment of such an agency if it is considered necessary. Until it is established, however, the disposition of tires from Brazil should remain subject to supervision by this Government, which is the only entity now in a position to provide that supervision.

9. The substance of the present arrangement is this: The Government of the country to which the tires are to be shipped issues a certificate of necessity to an importer in that country. The importer in turn forwards the certificate together with his order to an exporter either in Brazil or in this country. The exporter forwards an export application to the Office of Export Control of the Board of Economic Warfare and if the order is approved Rubber Reserve sells the tires to the exporter who carried out the transaction with the importer. The exporter thus has all the contracts with the importer in the normal commercial manner, the transaction merely being subject to approval of the export here not with respect to its business aspects but for the purpose of maintaining an equitable distribution of a scarce material.

You will note that orders can be placed either with Brazilian exporters or exporters in this country. The latter was included because importers of tires in the consuming countries were accustomed to deal with exporters in this country and Brazil has not heretofore been an exporter of tires. This latter fact of course means that it is not accurate for Brazil to talk about maintaining normal trade relations. Brazil actually wants to build up new relations; this Government naturally has no opposition to this objective. If agreement to continue purchase and distribution of Brazilian tires by Rubber Reserve could be achieved through exclusion of exporters in this country that would not be an insurmountable obstacle providing orders already placed and accepted by the Rubber Reserve from exporters in this country are executed.

If it would be more satisfactory to the Brazilian Government to have the application filed with the Rubber Reserve office in Rio de Janeiro that would be entirely acceptable here. Of course in that event, the applications would be forwarded to the Board of Economic Warfare here for consideration.

Rubber Reserve would also be entirely agreeable to making available to the appropriate Brazilian agencies information as to orders received, shipments made, etc.

10. In order to avoid implications of the kind referred to in paragraph 9 of the note from the Foreign office of 25 July 1942,[21] Brazil might notify the other Republics that the Government of Brazil and the US have agreed that there would be available, in Brazil or in the US, a specific quota for the next quarter and that such quotas might be obtained by following the procedures referred to above. In this way, Brazil would get credit for supplying the needs and at the same time the orders would be subjected to the controls regarded here as necessary. Quotas for the next quarter have been sent with Rubber Reserve's letter for 1 August to McAshan.

11. The substance of the foregoing is that it is desirable to continue the present arrangement, possibly excluding exporters in this country from the procedure and possibly providing for the filing of applications with the Rubber Reserve office in Rio. It is felt here that a change to the quota system administered by Brazil will result in a complete breakdown in the conservation program now well under way in the other American Republics.

Please inform McAshan and Micou of foregoing. It is concurred by Ambassador Caffery, Donnelly, Rubber Reserves and Board of Economic Warfare. (Please repeat to Allen)

HULL

• • • • •

811.20 (M) Brazil/1045: Telegram
The Charge in Brazil (Simmons) to the Secretary of State[22]
Rio de Janeiro, 15 August 1942, 1900 Hours
(Received 2205 Hours)

3069. For Cooke, Rubber Reserve from McAshan. Refer today's telephone conversation. As a result of numerous conferences Brazilian, Souza Costa's Commission proposes to confirm in writing their full agreement to the terms and methods set out in our letter to them of 10 August[23] copy airmailed you, provided that we agree to an exchange of notes between the Brazilian Foreign Office and American Embassy, Rio, setting out following conditions:

(1). Rubber Reserve will indicate monthly to the Commission for the Control of the Washington Agreements[24] the quantities of tires available that may be exported to the American Republics.

(2). By mutual agreement the Commission for Control of the Washington Agreements and Rubber Reserve will determine the countries to which these exportations shall be made, with the establishment also of the respective quantities.

(3). The exportation shall be made directly from exporter to importer, that is, through the normal channels of trade.

(4). The Government of Brazil shall have the exclusive responsibility of making the communication to those interested governments with respect of the quotas grated to each of them.

(5). For other manufactured rubber products which are or come to be manufactured in Brazil the Government of Brazil and the US agree to establish a plan to supply the other countries of this hemisphere under the same conditions established for tires and tubes.

They further read us their proposed announcement approximate translation being as follows:

"In accordance with the rubber agreement between Brazil and US dated March 3 which gives the US the right to purchase the entire exportable surplus of Brazilian crude and manufactured rubber, the Government of Brazil in cooperation with the US has arranged to assume a part of the responsibility of supplying the essential requirements of other American countries for those rubber manufactured articles which can best be made in Brazil and best shipped from Brazil. Quantities of such articles are to be made in advance on a quarterly basis to the countries of destination. The commitment for … quarter … year … for shipment from Brazil to the country will be … … passenger tires and tubes and truck tires and tubes."

Regarding condition number 2 above, the Brazilian Commission has agreed verbally to a full clearance with Washington in advance in order to follow Washington's global allotment for each country less the quantity, which can best be supplied from the US instead of Brazil. Although the Brazilian authorities have so far declined to put this specifically in the exchange of notes it may be possible to obtain such a commitment from them in a separate letter to our Embassy.

Regarding number 3 above, the Brazilian Commission has agreed on the Certificates of Necessity procedures in Department's telegram 2251, 12 August, provided certificates can be cleared through Rubber Reserve, Rio de Janeiro.

Micou has requested that above conditions particularly number 2 be cleared with Colonel Lord[25] and Peurifoy[26] for possible effect on Board of Economic Warfare program for allocating essential requirements to other American Countries.

We would appreciate your clearing the above counter proposal with interested Agencies and Departments in Washington and telegraphing or telephoning your instructions. (McAshan)

SIMMONS

• • • • •

811-20 Defense (M) Brazil/1084: Telegram
The Charge in Brazil (Simmons) to the Secretary of State[27]
Rio de Janeiro, 20 August 1942, 2100 Hours
(Received 21 August, 1242 Hours)

3166. For Cooke, Rubber Reserves, from McAshan. Discussed at length with Boucas late yesterday procedure for tire and tube exports. While he agrees to export price control and commits himself personally to accept allocations sent us in advance of each quarter by Washington, he cannot put in writing the fact that Brazil will follow quotas fixed by the US only. Furthermore, Commission entirely unwilling to agree that Certificates of Necessity be sent from Rio de Janeiro to Washington for processing but insists this be done here between Rubber Reserve representatives and Commission, with which we are inclined to agree.

They want a formal meeting with us to conclude this whole program by Monday at latest. Are we authorized conclude arrangements based on above, further that exchange of notes per our telegram 3069, 15 August, 1900 hours will take place promptly between Brazilian Foreign office and American Embassy, Rio?

SIMMONS

• • • • •

811.20 Defense (M)/1084: Telegram
The Secretary of State to Ambassador in Brazil (Caffery)[28]
Washington, 21 August 1942, 2300 Hours

2396. For McAshan. Your letter 341, 10 August,[29] and telegrams 3069, 15 August 3166, 20 August. Following are conclusions after further discussions by Department, Board of Economic Warfare, Rubber Reserve and Donnelly, for which please try to secure Brazilian acceptance.

1st: If Brazilian tires are to be distributed equally and on basis of indispensable needs, agreement on all transactions should be obtained from Washington. It is suggested that applications and orders be presented by the Commission for the control of Washington Agreements to Rubber Reserve, Rio de Janeiro. The latter can then informally advise Rubber Reserve, Washington, by telegraph or otherwise of facts necessary for passing judgment. The agreement between the two Governments needs not, of course, refer to anything except approval by Rubber Reserve, Rio de Janeiro it is believed here that, through special arrangements with Board of Economic Warfare, each transaction could be processed here within 48 hours of receipt. The reason for this procedure is that there is believed to be only insufficient information in Rio de Janeiro for adequate consideration of the applications to be expected. It does not have the names of the people on the Proclaimed List in the other countries; this list changes from day to day. It is not in a position to pass on the importance of particular projects for which tires may be needed; Washington has detailed information as to the purpose and status of these projects.

2nd: Washington should have the right to approve and if need be to direct allocations. It has made commitments to the other American Republics. A general commitment was made in the Department's circular telegram of 18 May[30] and in all agreements with the rubber producing countries this Government has agreed to use its best efforts to supply specified tonnages of rubber products. In addition, this Government has agreed with certain of the countries to furnish specific numbers of tires. In agreement with Colombia, for instance, this Government undertook to supply 20,000 tires immediately and 30,000 tires within a year. Emergency allocations were made to Peru, Chile and the Dominican Republic in specific amounts. In making these allocations, this Government relied on the availability of Brazilian tires. What happens if the disposition of Brazilian tires is not in accord with our commitments?

Further we do not know whether Brazil could withstand the anticipated diplomatic and domestic pressure, and believe that it may find it advantageous to be relieved from it.

We regret that it therefore seems impossible, to concur in the proposed procedure. It is suggested that, if possible, you delay any final action until Donnelly's return; he is fully informed as to our position and concurs in it.

HULL

• • • • •

811.20 Defense (M) Brazil/1182: Telegram
The Ambassador in Brazil (Caffery) to the Secretary of State[31]
Rio de Janeiro—31 August 1942, 0000 Hours
(Received 1-6 September, (8 a.m.)

3343. For Levy,[32] Cooke, Bicknell, from Hays, Micou, McAshlan. Boucas Commission agreed this evening to recommend to the ministers of Foreign Affairs and Finance[33] an exchange of notes between the Brazilian Foreign office and the American Embassy Rio as follows:

1: Considering the Agreement of 3 March, signed in Washington between Brazil and the US, by which the American Government agreed to acquire from Brazil all of the exportable surplus of crude and manufactured rubber, and considering further that, within the spirit evidenced at the Third Conference of Foreign Ministers of the American Republics, there exists a necessity for real cooperation between all of the countries of the Americas, the Governments of Brazil and the US resolve to establish, by mutual agreement, a system for determining the allocation for supplying tires and tubes to the nations of the Western Hemisphere.

2: For the purpose of taking care of the wartime requirements and having in mind the defense of the Americas, within an over-all plan of supply, the American Government, using the statistical services which it has at its disposal to determine the requirements of the American Republics, relative to tires and tubes will propose to Brazil the allocations which Brazil should supply to the other American Republics.

3. On these conditions, periodically and by mutual agreement with the US, Brazil will make known directly, to the other interested countries the allocations fixed for each quarter.

4. Exportation will be made directly from exporter to importer, namely, in the normal channels of trade.

5. For other rubber manufactured articles, which are or may be produced in Brazil, the Government of Brazil and the US mutually agree to establish a place (plan?) for supplying the nations of this hemisphere following the same methods established for tires and tubes."

We are not positive that the Minister of Foreign Relations will accept the last sentence of paragraph 2 quoted above, but the Control Commission is so recommending. May we confirm to them officially that you accept the above working for an exchange of notes establishing the conditions governing the mechanics of the exportation of manufactured rubber products from Brazil under the main Rubber Agreement of 3 March?

If so, please be prepared to cable us the allocations of the third and fourth quarters of 1942 covering tires and tubes to be supplied from Brazil to each other Western hemisphere country, for prompt submission to the Brazilian authorities as soon as they confirm their acceptance.[34]

Boucas Commission has also agreed to write a separate letter confirming that Certificates of necessity will be submitted to Rubber Reserve Rio for approval before any export permits will be granted, and Rubber Reserve. Rio will have time to clear all such certificates with Washington by cable. Further, the Boucas Commission will confirm to us in that separate letter that exporter's resale prices to other American countries will not be more than ten percent above the price at which Rubber Reserve releases tires and tubes stocks to those exporters, both based f.o.b. steamer Brazilian ports. (Hays, Micou, McAshan)

CAFFERY

After weeks of back and forth wrangling between the highest-ranking officials in both governments, there was finally an agreement. Both sides had to give a little on various points, but when the Brazilians made it clear that they did not want the world to think they were being controlled by the US government, the US officials finally found a way to satisfy the Brazilians and move forward. It may have been the most critical moment in a protracted negotiation for Brazilian rubber, which began 3 March 1942, and stretched into the month of September, finally resolving the issues of a monumental agreement between both countries, which ultimately provided the critical rubber needed to win World War II.

CHAPTER 12

THE TIPPING POINT

What may have been the tipping point in the final decision to support the United States (US) and its Allies occurred in August 1942. German U-boats sank six Brazilian passenger and cargo ships off the northeastern coast, killing many civilians, including women and children. U-boat attacks on Brazilian commercial shipping interrupted food supplies from southern Brazil to the Amazon, and the northeast, causing serious food shortages. Having assumed responsibility for food as well as health programs under the Washington accords, Nelson Rockefeller's Coordinator of Inter-American Affairs (CIAA) responded quickly by negotiating a technical assistance agreement with Brazil to improve food production methods in the northeast, with the goal of reducing its dependence on basic foods from the south.[1]

With North American troops stationed in a string of military bases along Brazil's northeastern coast, the Roosevelt administration's policy was to help the region through this wartime food crisis. Southern Brazil traditionally supplied the Amazon with basic foods, including wheat, corn, meat, coffee, sugar, and cooking oils, while receiving natural rubber, minerals and forest products in exchange. Except for Marajo, Bragantina, and a few other regions of Para, the Amazon did not produce food on a commercial scale. Due to constant threats of U-boat attacks on maritime shipping, commerce between southern and northern Brazil became sporadic and unreliable, prices of food soared in the Amazon, and shortages became acute. Even Manaus suffered wartime food shortages. The Rubber Development Corporation (RDC) and Superinten-

Stocks of Food Maintained by the RDC and SAVA. *National Archives Building, Washington, DC (NAB)*

dencia para el Abastecimiento del Valle Amazónico (SAVA) agreed to cooperate in maintaining stocks of essential basic foods and supplies in Amazonian ports including: sugar, rice, coffee, lard, salt, wheat, tobacco, matches, beef jerky, axes, knives, headlamp, kerosene, fishhooks, rifles, gunpowder and cloth. No roads connected southern Brail or any other region of the country with the Amazon. Protected by military convoys, supplies traveled along the Atlantic coast to Belém.[2]

The agreements between the US and the Vargas governments, which restricted the use of natural rubber for anything but the war effort met with a great deal of resistance in the Brazilian market. Manufacturers, who had developed many other rubber products such as toys, cut thread, shoes and the like, were extremely disappointed by the restrictions agreed upon between the Vargas and the Roosevelt governments. The agreement covering these restrictions was explicate and the United States insisted on strict adherence. The US itself was no exception, as every pound of rubber extracted from the Amazon was used to bolster the war effort.

• • • • •

811.20 Defense (M) Brazil/1355a: Telegram
The Secretary of State to the Ambassador in Brazil (Caffery)[3]
Washington, 15 September 1942, 2200 Hours

272. It is considered urgent here that immediate agreement be reached with the Brazilian Government for the establishment of mutually satisfactory prices for the purchase of rubber products by the US (presumably Rubber Reserve Company) as contemplated by paragraph 7 of the Rubber Agreement of 3 March. Prices have been established for the purchase of tires but we think we should now endeavor to establish prices for other manufactured rubber products.

There has been correspondence between Korkegi[4] and Rubber Reserve regarding the problem of curtailing production of nonessential rubber products such as rubber thread, rubber toys and the like. The present object of the Rubber Reserve and BEW[5] is not only to obtain the cooperation of the Brazilian Government in the curtailment of the manufacture of nonessential rubber products but also to assist in the conversion of existing facilities to the production of essential rubber products. To this end Rubber Reserve stands ready to purchase existing surplus stocks of manufactured rubber products held by manufacturers and upon specific recommendations of the US Purchasing Commission in Brazil, and assuming that such curtailment can be accomplished, Rubber Reserve will help in the conversion depending upon the merit in each case.

Some system of control should be established by the Brazilian Government to restrict so far as possible the manufacture of miscellaneous rubber goods except tires and the possible prohibition of the manufacture of nonessentials such as cut thread, toys and the like. It would seem appropriate that the Brazilian Government exercise the suggested control of the allocation of crude rubber to the manufacturers and that the appropriate agency of this Government assist in such control by the licensing of shipments of chemicals and supplies to such manufacturers from this country.

That this matter is of great urgency is shown by Korkegi's reports that the manufacture of nonessential rubber products in Brazil is definitely on the increase, as illustrated by an account of the increase of the production of rubber thread in the case of one manufacturer from eight hundred kilograms to one thousand four hundred kilograms per day, and that the present exportable surplus of rubber thread alone is estimated at thirty five tons per month.

HULL

• • • • •

811.20 Defense (M) Brazil/1521
The Assistant Chief of the Division of Defense Materials (Cissel)
To the Chief of the Division of the American Republics (Bonsal)[6]
Washington, 2 October 1942

Mr Bonsal: Telegram 3937, 1 October from Rio[7] requested that we telephone Donnelly and Russell[8] with respect to the tire and tube agreement. This was done this morning. Donnelly advised that they had had an extended conference with the Foreign Minister yesterday and had obtained complete agreement on the tire and tube contract in the form submitted by Allen with the changes requested in the Department's telegram of 24 September.[9] Several additional changes were suggested by Aranha. Most important was as follows:

The agreement now provides that twenty-five percent of the tires manufactured in Brazil will be sold to the US. Brazil wishes the right to increase or decrease this figure, so long as the manufacture does not exceed ten thousand tons. Donnelly stated that the Foreign minister had made a very strong statement to the effect that strict conservation of tires would be instituted in Brazil and that in his opinion it is unwise to attempt to get a better arrangement on this point. In view of this and in view of the fact that the lack of petroleum has automatically reduced the use of tires in Brazil, it was decided to accept the proposal.

The other changes were accepted and Donnelly was instructed, with the concurrence of Rubber Reserve Company, Board of Economic Warfare and myself on behalf of the Department to proceed with the execution of the agreement,[10] which is expected this afternoon or tomorrow morning.

While the subject was not mentioned specifically, I gathered from the telephone conversation that any difficulty with respect to Boucas' proposed resignation had been eliminated.

• • • • •

832.796/103: Telegram
The Ambassador in Brazil (Caffery) to the Secretary of State[11]
Rio de Janeiro, 3 October 1942, 1700 Hours
(Received 2300 Hours)

3970. Department's 2894, 30 September, 2300 hours.[12] As reported in my telegraph of 3841 of 26 September, 1700 hours, permission was officially granted for route Miami-Manaus. No contract between Defense Suppliers Corporation and Brazilian Government for this service is necessary and Defense Supplies Corporation may proceed to make contact with carrier.

We are awaiting expected favorable action from Air Minister[13] on routes Para—Iquitos and Manaus-Guajara Mirim. This will authorize Defense Supplies Corporation to contact with any Brazilian airline it desires for these routes. As in the case of the Manaus-Miami route no contact between the Defense Supplies Corporation and Brazilian Government is necessary.

As soon as the general agreement covering air transportation for the rubber program is approved (this will probably be delayed 1 week because of Air Minister's absence in Buenos Aires), the Ministry of Air will name officials of Defense Supplies Corporation and Rubber Reserve in these cities, on the basis of the general agreement. By details, are meant specific approval for the construction of airports at mutually selected sites, et cetera.

The entire matter of the agreement covering air transportation activities for the rubber program has been carried out directly by the Ministry of Air, as a step implementing the rubber agreement signed in Washington 3 March. Minister for Air and Finance Ministry is unnecessary, and the Embassy believes insistence on such a procedure might complicate and delay matters.

A copy and translation of the draft agreement which has been favorably reported by the Director of Civil Aviation[14] (it is also agreeable to Boucas and the Minister of Finance), and is awaiting final sanction by the Minister for Air, is brought forwarded by air mail today.[15]

Caffery

• • • • •

811.20 Defense (M) Brazil/1764a: Telegram
The Secretary of State to the Ambassador in Brazil (Caffery)[16]
Washington, 27 October 1942, 2200 Hours.

3259. Your 4325 of 22 October, 1500 hours.[17] The Department and the other interested agencies in Washington will be glad to examine jointly with the Brazilian and Uruguayan Governments the tire requirements of Uruguay as estimated by the Uruguayan authorities.

With regard to other countries such as Colombia, Venezuela, Peru, Ecuador and Bolivia the allocations were reached by agreement between the governments of those countries in each case with the US. The resentment in the other American republics arises from the delay in shipping the agreed allocations; this delay is caused solely by the protracted negotiations and delays in Rio. Argentina had offered gleefully to enter agreements to supply tires to Ecuador, etc. In case, we fail to fulfill our obligations.

The Department understands that the Uruguayan case may be a special one, for political or other reasons of importance to Brazil; but before "reconsideration of the entire tire allocation plan" we would like to have specific information from you whether the Brazilian resentment is against the several bilateral tire allocation agreements, mentioned above; or whether you are recommending at the insistence of the Brazilian Government to scrap and negotiate again the agreement in the exchange of notes of 3 October 1942 (enclosures 4 and 8 of your dispatch 8678 of 7 October 1942),[18] especially paragraphs 1 and 5.

The joint objectives of the Brazilians and the US Government in the general agreement of 3 March 1942 and the manufactured rubber good agreement of 3 October 1942 was to make the maximum of critically needed rubber available to the joint war effort without sacrifice to the essential needs of the other American republics (which are to be supplied from the most accessible source).

You will, we are sure, understand why the Department is loath to have "the entire tire allocation plan" reconsidered. If nevertheless you still think the Brazilians have valid objections, please furnish the Department the full story.

HULL

• • • • •

811.20 Defense (M) Brazil/1872: Telegram
The Ambassador in Brazil (Caffery) to the Secretary of State[19]
Rio de Janeiro, 12 November 1942, 1900 Hours
(Received 2155 Hours)

4721. For Duggan.[20] My telegram No. 4608, 7 November, 1600 hours.[21] The Venezuelan Ambassador called yesterday to say he had received a telegram from the President of Venezuela instructing him to arrange for the immediate shipment of tires and tubes to Venezuela. The Ambassador was surprised to learn from the Foreign Officer that there was no allocation for his country for the fourth quarter and inquired if this was correct. I told him that one of my experts would call on him to explain the situation.

The tire and tube situation here is unsatisfactory. It is evident that unless we can assure the Foreign Minister that each American country has agreed to the allocation that it is not unilateral action on our part, the Foreign Office will be under constant pressure from representatives of American Republics here and will not be in a position to justify the allocations. This may lead to the repudiation of the agreement to the extent that the Brazilian Government will authorize the exportation of tires and tubes to other countries independent of the allocation.

The Department's telegram 3021, 10 October,[22] it was implied that allocations of tires and tubes to a number of countries had either been reached by agreement or in the case of certain countries with whom the US has rubber agreements, the allocation represented the amount stimulated (stipulated) in such agreement to cover internal consumption. If such is the case, it is amply apparent from statements made by the Ambassadors of these countries in Brazil that neither they nor their governments understand the situation.

Aside from its effects on Brazil, it would seem desirable that the US endeavor to arrive at allocations by consultation and agreement with each country.

Aranha has instructed the Commission for Control of Washington Agreements to "insist with the American authorities here" that Uruguay and Venezuela receive allocations for the fourth quarter for four thousand and five thousand tires and tubes, respectively.

I have observed an increasing resentment on the part of my American colleagues here to what they call "arbitrary" action of our Government in dictating the allocations and products they may receive from Brazil.

Caffery

• • • • •

811.20 Defense (M) Brazil/1908: Telegram
The Ambassador in Brazil (Caffery) to the Secretary of State[23]
Rio de Janeiro, 16 November 1942, 1800 Hours
(Received 2328 Hours)

4784. My telegram No. 2237, 26 June, 1600 hours.[24] Souza Costa told me yesterday that Aranha is determined to ship the six hundred tons of crude rubber to Chile which he promised the Chilean Government during the Pan-American Conference here in January and which he alleges was approved by our Government; also the Chilean Embassy here has already acquired ninety tons for prompt shipment to Chile. Costa said he had strongly opposed the proposed sale of the rubber to Chile on the ground that it violated the rubber agreement with the US, but that Aranha has taken the position that it is an agreement between two governments and that he as Minister of Foreign Affairs committed the Brazilian Government and that therefore Costa as Minister of Finance has nothing to do with it.

Aranha told Souza Costa that he would resign rather than to break his agreement with Chilean Government. We are reliably informed that the Chileans have had no success in buying additional crude rubber in Brazil and that Aranha is so aroused he might even compel firms to meet the requirements of Chile. Alan and I have reviewed the situation and feel that we should obtain factual information regarding the cruder rubber requirements of Chile and recent purchases of crude rubber by Chile from Bolivia and other countries. If we can clearly establish that Chile's requirements of crude rubber, taking into consideration the consumption of manufacturing equipment now available there does not exceed one hundred tons annually, which is Allen's recollection, we could use this point most effectively in our discussions with Aranha and follow-up with the obvious observation that the excess of five hundred tons might find its way to Argentina tires and tubes and other essentials. It would assist if we could assure Aranha that Chile has been given a specific assurance that their essential requirements of tires and tubes or other essential products will be supplied from the US or Brazil. These points could be used to supplement our basic contention that in the absence of any specific exception in the basic rubber agreement of 3 March 1942, that any outstanding commitments on that date on the part of Brazil were nullified.

I have no recollection of the US Government at any time giving its express or implied approval to the reported transaction between Brazil and Chile, but I would like to have the Departments specific assurance in this regard.

CAFFERY

• • • • •

811.20 Defense (M) Brazil/1908: Telegram
The Secretary of State to the Ambassador in Brazil (Caffery)[25]
Washington, 24 November 1942, 2100 Hours.

3672. Embassy's 4784, 16 November. Chile's stocks crude rubber recently estimated at four hundred to five hundred tons. Pre-war normal consumption was approximately four hundred tons per year including many non-essential items production of which is no longer permitted in this country and is discouraged in Brazil. It is estimated here that Chile's requirements crude rubbers for essentials do not exceed two hundred tons per year including thirty five tons for retreading. Chile is not to receive machinery from this country for the manufacture of tires. Department is telegraphing Santiago to check Washington's requirement estimates and details of Chile's recent imports. This information will be telegraphed to you. In any case, it would be deplorable were Chile to receive additional six hundred tons from Brazil, an excess which no doubt would be re-exported to Argentina as evidenced by a pending transaction in which Corporación de Fomento, Chile, is to supply crude rubber to Pirelli,[26] Argentina and receive a return of fifty percent by weight in bicycle tires. Assurance to supply Chile's essential requirements conveyed to Child in Department's circular telegraph of 18 May,[27] and reiterated in Department's telegram to our Embassy which announced third quarter emergency allocation available from Brazil, stating that orders placed under this allocation would supersede orders previously placed in Brazil. An attempt will be made to reach an understanding with Chilean authorities regarding Chile's rubber requirements and use this understanding s basis for future allocations.

You have Departments assurance that this government at no time approved sale of rubber by Brazil to Chile except to fulfill Chile's essential wartime requirements under the usual allocation procedure.

HULL

• • • • •

811.20 Defense (M) Brazil 20454½
Memorandum by Mr Arthur A. Compton, Division of the American Republics, to the Adviser on Political Relations (Duggan)[28]
Washington, 1 December 1942

Mr Duggan; At your request I have gone over the attached material[29] relating to the arrangements we have under our various rubber agreements to supply the needs of other American republics for raw rubber or rubber manufactured goods. Although incomplete, the attached material reveals a story somewhat as follows:

1. Immediately after the basic rubber agreements of 3 March with Brazil, the US was compelled to purchase all of the existing stocks and future output of manufactured rubber from Brazil in order to prevent a big boom in Brazilian rubber manufacture and indiscriminate export to the other American republics. In the specific negotiations for this purchase and contract, it was agreed that exportable surpluses of tires, tubes and miscellaneous rubber goods should be used (at least in part) for supplying the essential requirements for those items to the other American republics as agreed in the contracts made with other rubber producing countries in the hemisphere. In consideration of this provision, Brazil agreed to reduce its rubber manufacture and its internal consumption of manufactured rubber goods in order to leave more raw rubber for export to the US.

2. It is then agreed that the method of supplying the essential needs of the other American republics for raw and manufactured rubber from both the US and the Brazil would be as follows:

(a) The US would determine on the basis of the statistics available to it the quarterly allocations of manufactured rubber goods to supply the essential needs of the other American republics

(b) Brazil would announce those allocations

(c) The other American republics could then proceed to purchase (with the allocation announced) from either the US or the Brazil, their essential manufactured rubber goods through the regular commercial channels.

(d) Control over these purchases is to be maintained through clearance with the Rubber Reserve Company in Washington of all purchases from either Brazil or the US (the actual granting of the certificate permitting export being in the hands of the government of the country from which the rubber is to be exported).

3. The foregoing procedures have given rise to the difficulties outlined in the Ambassador's telegrams 4325 of 22 October, 1500 hours[30] and 4721 of 12 November, 1900 hours directed to you personally. It is my feeling that although both internal Brazilian politics and policies played by other American republics have a large part in these difficulties; the major problems would be solved if we could accomplish two things:

(a) It is necessary to make available to the Brazilian Government the information used in arriving at the allocations established by us for the other American republics in order that the Brazilian Government may be in a position to defend these allocations (which they announced) against the inroads of political pressure from the other American republics.

(b) It is further of the greatest importance in reducing the political pressure from the other Americas (which thrives and grows on misunderstandings and delays) or provide for the complete and definite understanding (as far in advance as possible) by each of the other Americas of the quarterly allocations applying to them and to provide to the greatest extent possible for the rapid and efficient delivery of rubber purchased by each of the other Americas under these allocations.

4. Although I am not in a position to recommend the specific technical details of how these ends should be accomplished, I would recommend by way of suggestion that every consideration be given to the following possibilities:

a. The establishment in Washington of a joint Brazilian-US rubber commission, which among other things would serve the following purposes:

i. It would serve as a source of information to the Brazilian Government on the statistics and considerations involved in arriving at the final rubber allocations so that the Brazilian Government would be in a position to defend these allocations which they are now obliged to announce

ii. It would serve also as a body, which could arbitrate any difficulties or differences of opinion as to these allocations, which may be raised in Brazil by any of the other American republics (in this connection, any statistics available to Brazil, which do not coincide with ours would be useful in bringing to light any possible misinformation on which our own statistic may be based).

b. The careful consideration is strongly urged of the possibility of consulting the governments of the other American republics as to what they believe their essential rubber requirements are. These estimates and their justifications could then be examined in the light of the information available to the US (supplemented by any information available to Brazil) and altered or cut down accordingly. This procedure would, to my way of thinking, put us in a much firmer position as regards our justification for "dictating" to the other Americas what their needs are. They would then at least feel that they had had a chance to present their story. This to me seems most important.

c. The working out a clear procedure for the joint announcement by the US and Brazil (perhaps by the suggested joint commission) of the quarterly allocations applying to each of the other Americas in such a way that no misunderstanding will be possible as to the actual amounts of these allocations and as much explanation thereof as may be possible in order to satisfy any complaints which may be received with respect to these allocations.

d. The provision in so far as possible of a clearly understood and efficiently operating delivery service both from the US and from Brazil for the rubber goods purchased under these rubber allocations.

Note: The foregoing comments are intended to apply to the ultimate ironing out of the long-range difficulties, which seem to be involved in the present rubber arrangements. As regards the specific problems of Uruguay, Venezuela, Chile, etc. raised in Ambassador Caffery's wires to you, I believe they will have to be ironed out as well as may be possible by whatever specific action can be taken immediately.

> In this connection, it is interesting to note that we are not even sure that all of the announcements of the fourth quarter allocations have yet been made even though we are now entering into the last month of the fourth quarter. It is further pointed out that deliveries have not yet been made on all of the third quarter allocation. Such delays have lent fuel to the present flare-up and serve to emphasize the necessity of immediate farsighted action to apply to the announcement and prompt delivery of the allocations for the forthcoming year. Actually, these announcements should already have been made and each day that goes by creates potential difficulties for next year.

Although the US and Brazil had seemingly ironed out all of the questions in the original accords, beginning with the accord of 3 March 1942, as well as the questions and challenges raised at the Third Conference of the American Republics in Rio in January 1942, as the war progressed, more and more difficulties arose. In the first place, the American republics, specifically the Argentines, Venezuelans and Chileans were unhappy with the allocations of rubber products they received from the US lead commission. Even US supporter, Oswaldo Aranha, Brazilian foreign minister, questioned the US resistance to allowing Chile to have more rubber and rubber products than the US felt they needed. The US had the concern that Chile would sell part of their allocation to Argentina, which was an Axis ally, and that this rubber would turn into tubes and tires which would be sold to the Germans and the Italians.

Brazilian Foreign Minister, Aranha, who had been a staunch supporter of the US agenda in the Rio conference, felt that it was important that Brazil maintain its commitment, not only to Chile, but to the other American republics as well. So, firm was he in this position that he threatened to resign as foreign minister if the issue was not resolved to his satisfaction.

The communiqués in this chapter between the US Secretary of State and the US officials in Rio clearly demonstrate the frustration on both sides.

CHAPTER 13
THE UNITED STATES BECOMES COMMITTED

The following communication between the United States (US) Secretary of State and the US Ambassador in Brazil laid the groundwork for US involvement in the transportation of around fifty thousand rubber soldiers from the Brazilian northeast to the rubber plantations of the Amazon basin. As part of the agreement with Brazilian President Vargas, the US also authorized the transportation of tons of food into the region to improve the conditions and nutrition of the rubber soldiers. All of this became necessary as the German U-boat threat along the northeastern coast of Brazil increased, and Brazil's merchant ships were being attacked.

• • • • •

811.20 Defense (M) Brazil 2243a: Telegram
The Secretary of State to the Ambassador in Brazil (Caffery)[1]
Washington, 26 December 1942, 1600 Hours
4060. For Russell, Donelly from Allen. This will confirm telephone conversation advising you that that the text of the agreement between Rubber Reserve and Worker Mobilization Service in the Amazon (SEMTA,[2] Servigo de Mobilizagao de Trabalhadores para Amazonia) had been approved by the Board of Economic Warfare, Rubber Reserve and State Department with a few slight changes given you over the telephone and

Joao Alberto Luis de Barros in Manaus. *National Archives Building, Washington, DC (NAB)*

authorizing you to sign the agreement. We also confirm authority to provide up to one hundred fifty thousand dollars for construction of reception and other facilities for whatever organization of the Brazilian Government undertakes the responsibility of caring for and placing the labor transported into the Amazon by SEMTA. You are also authorized to purchase up to twenty five thousand tons of staple foodstuffs to create a food reserve in the Amazon. You are also authorized to lease such additional storage facilities at Belém, Manaus or other points on the Amazon for storage of foodstuffs, rubber supplies and equipment. Suggest endeavor to transport to the Amazon not less than fifteen thousand tons of foodstuffs within the next thirty days and entire quantity by 15 February. We have discussed with João Alberto the equipment needed for the movement of fifty thousand workers by SEMTA and their transportation on the Tocantins River and we have arranged for a large number of shallow draft boats suitable for transporting labor, which can be used on the Tocantins and also on the San Francisco and Parnahyba Rivers. I am planning to arrive in Belém around 1 or 2 January and João Alberto[3] is planning to arrive around 8 January and expects to spend a few days at Belém. Suggest desirability of Boucas and Doria being available at Belém at that time. (Allen)

HULL

• • • • •

811.20 Defense (M) Brazil/2130: Telegram
The Secretary of State to the Ambassador in Brazil (Caffery)[4]
Washington, 26 December 1942, 1900 Hours

4063. Embassy's 5334, 15 December.[5] Department approves the form of agreement with the changes agreed upon by Allen and Donnelly in telephone conversation on 17 December.

Before operations are undertaken under the agreement, it is believed advisable that Embassy secure clear understanding of the following matters:

1. As to the methods that will be used for recruiting the labor in question.

2. As to the fact that the labor obtained shall be placed in employment through an agency of the Brazilian Government and that the Brazilian Government will hold itself responsible for the working conditions of the laborers and the terms of the labor contracts that may be entered into. These of course should be discussed with the Rubber Reserve Company.

3. That the Brazilian Government will take all necessary measures so that suitable reception and arrangements are worked out for handling the laborers upon their arrival in Belém and their eventual placement in the producing areas with such financial and technical advice from the Rubber Reserve as may be requested.

The Department's approval of the arrangement is based on the belief that the rubber shortage is so serious and has such military importance as to justify emergency arrangements of this kind. Nevertheless it is felt that the local representatives of the Rubber Reserve Company must follow its execution extremely closely and that the Embassy should at all times keep itself fully informed and satisfy itself that this whole program is being carried out in such a way as to avoid the grave consequences which might otherwise ensue.

HULL

The communiqué above may be one of the most significant communiqués in the first years of World War II, as it defines perfectly the US's understanding of the responsibilities of both countries. The US agreed to provide not only transportation and food supplies for the rubber soldiers, but in earlier agreements five million dollars in cash to build the infrastructure of the new rubber venture.

• • • • •

811.20 Defense (M) Brazil /2236: Telegram
The Ambassador in Brazil (Caffery) to the Secretary of State[6]
Rio de Janeiro, 28 December 1942, 1800 Hours
(Received 2045 Hours)

5509. Department's 4063, 6 (26) December, 1900 Hours

(1). The laborers will be recruited by SEMTA. Brazilian Government officials are now organizing the program.

(2) The Brazilian Government will be responsible for the working conditions of the laborers, the terms of labor contacts, et cetera, and the laborers will be placed in employment through an agency of the Brazilian Government. All of these points have been cleared with the Rubber Reserve Company.

(3). Reception facilities, housing, supplies of foodstuffs, medicines, et cetera, at Para will be handled by agencies of the Brazilian Government and the Rubber Reserve's responsibility will be restricted to financial and technical advice as may be requested. The Embassy and the Rubber Reserve Company here will follow the execution of the plan extremely closely. A representative of the Rubber Reserve will make periodic trips to the labor recruiting areas, Belém and the Amazon River will keep the Embassy currently informed of the progress of the work.

CAFFERY

• • • • •

811.20 Defense (M) Brazil/1908: Telegram
The Secretary of State to the Ambassador in Brazil (Caffery)[7]
Washington, 12 January 1943, 1800 Hours

122. Department's 3672, 24 November. Department has been advised by Embassy at Santiago that fifty thousand, two hundred forty-seven kilograms washed crude rubber arrived Valparaiso 13 December, consigned to Corporación de Fomento, shipped from Santos, Brazil, November 17, by Arthur Dianna y Compañía Limitada.

The Department's information on Chile's crude rubber supply and demand was contained in Department's 3672, 24 November.

The shipment referred to is in violation of the rubber agreement. As indicated in Department's 3672, it consists of rubber not needed by Chile and at least part of which will probably reach Argentina in finished form.

Under the circumstances, you are requested to take the matter up with the Minister of Foreign Affairs expressing the view that the shipment violated the rubber agreement and protesting such violation, especially when Chile has no justifiable need for the rubber and when Brazil and this Government have undertaken to supply and are now supplying Chile's needs for tires and other rubber products.

HULL

CHAPTER 14

THE HIGH PRICE OF RUBBER

By the end of 1943, there began to be some concerns in Washington about the effectiveness of the Amazon rubber campaign. The cost in both money and human lives was becoming a real concern to many United States (US) officials. The other main concern was whether the Amazon campaign could ever produce enough rubber to satisfy the needs of the war effort. Certainly, the initiative was critical to bolster US rubber stocks at the outset of the war, but whether enough rubber could be produced to satisfy all of the mounting requirements, was becoming a big question.

In spite of the fifty thousand rubber tappers sent to the Amazon from the Brazilian northeast by the Vargas government, production was falling short of the long-term goals. In 1941, Brazil only produced sixteen thousand three hundred seventeen tons of rubber and the US was hoping, after an extensive survey, that the fifty thousand rubber tappers could produce fifty thousand tons of rubber. In reality, the tappers could only produce approximately half-ton each per year and this was even above the average.

The US began an aggressive recycled rubber campaign and accelerated its quest for synthetic rubber. US scientists and government officials reasoned that although natural rubber was the preferred product, it was becoming more and more apparent that the demand was far exceeding the Amazon's ability to supply and synthetic rubber would have to be the ultimate answer.

• • • • •

DISCUSSIONS AND AGREEMENTS BETWEEN THE UNITED STATES AND BRAZIL ON RUBBER PRICES, QUOTAS, AND THE INTRODUCTION OF SYNTHETIC RUBBER INTO BRAZIL

102.8951 Rio de Janeiro: Airgram
The Secretary of State to the Ambassador in Brazil (Caffery)[2]
Washington, 28 January 1944, 0040 Hours.

A-105 For McAshan[3] from Allen[4] Rubber Development Corporation (RDC). Following is the text of an agreement, reached with Bocus,[5] which he has accepted on behalf of the Government of Brazil. This Agreement has likewise been ratified by the Directors of RDC.

"Dear Mr Boucas: I have the honor to record in this note that, as a result of conversations between you, in your capacity as Executive Director of the Commission for the Control of Washington Accords, and as authorized representative of the Government of Brazil, and myself, in my capacity as President of RDC, the following has been agreed upon between the Government of Brazil and the RDC:

1) RDC agrees to pay a premium of thirty-three and a third percent over the "Fixed Price" as set forth in the agreement dated 3 March 1942[6] between RDC (as successor to Rubber Reserve Company) and Government of Brazil and as supplemented by the Supplemental Agreement dated 29 September 1943, which established the "Fixed Price" (referred to in the Supplemental Agreement as the "basic price") at forty five cents per pound f.o.b. Belém for Acre, fine, washed and dried, said premium to be payable upon rubber which is available for quality inspection or has been inspected for RDC at an agreed shipping port and which has been tendered by the Banco de Crédito da Borracha to RDC for purchase during the period commencing with a date (subsequent hereto) to be agreed upon by Brazil and RDC and ending 31 March 1945; it being understood that all rubber tendered thereafter to RDC under the aforesaid agreements shall be purchased at the "Fixed Price" therein established (i.e., on the basis of forty five cents per pound f.o.b. Belém for Acre fine, washed and dried) without payment of the above mentioned premium, unless the Government of Brazil and the RDC shall have executed a written agreement for a continuance of the premium thereafter.

2) In view of the fact that RDC is paying the premium above referred to in order (a) to offset increased wages, living costs and other items affecting the cost of rubber production and (b) to provide stimulus to maximum production, it is understood and agreed that RDC shall discontinue at the earliest practicable date gradually and in accord with the Commission for the Control of the Washington Accords, but in any case not later than 30 June 1944, all payments, subsidies and contributions for these purposes, except for obligations already incurred by RDC Corporation under the CAETA[7] Agreement,[8] and Brazil agrees to the cancelation or modification of such provisions of any agreements between RDC and Government of Brazil (or any agency or corporation instrumentality thereof) as may be necessary to be canceled or modified in order to relieve RDC of such payments, subsidies and contributions. Among other things the Government of Brazil agrees to a termination at such earliest practicable date of the following specific commitments and obligations of RDC:

1) Any obligations to supply staple foodstuffs or to maintain fixed prices therefore under the agreement dated 3 April 1943[9] between RDC and Superintendência de Abastecimento do Vale Amazônico (SAVA).

2) Any obligation to make available at less than cost tappers' supplies and equipment under the aforesaid agreement between RDC and SAVA.

Any obligation under the proposed agreement dated 16 July 1943 between RDC and Amazon Navigational and Administrational Service of the Port of Pará (SNAPP, Serviço de Navegação e Administração dos Portos do Pará) to provide coal at less than cost or to pay higher than estimated freight rates on freight of RDC moved by SNAPP on vessels other than those owned by RDC furnished by RDC to SNAPP.

3. In view of the fact that RDC has already expended in furtherance of the wild rubber program in Brazil amounts substantially in excess of five million dollars development fund contemplated in the agreement of 3 March 1942, Brazil agrees to assume all development expenditures that may be required from now on, using for this purpose the volume premiums payable by RDC to Brazil in accordance with paragraph 4 of the aforesaid agreement of 3 March 1942 and such other funds as the Government of Brazil may make available for such purpose.

Among other things Brazil specifically agrees to assume all future development expenditures with respect to the following:

a. Road building activities in Southern Mato Grosso.

b. Labor subsidy in Southern Mato Grosso.

4. In accordance with Paragraph 5 of the agreement of 3 March 1942 Brazil agrees to take such action as may be necessary to require consumers of rubber within Brazil to pay the "Fixed Price," plus the above mentioned premium of thirty-three and a third percent, so that the export and internal prices of rubber shall be the same.

It is further understood and agreed that the price heretofore agreed upon by the RDC and Brazil for the exportable surplus of tires and tubes which has been sold to RDC under the provision of the agreement of 3 October 1942,[10] shall not be increased as a result of the premium herein provided for unless it can be demonstrated that the manufacturers thereof cannot operate at a reasonable margin of profit, in which case Brazil and RDC shall consult together and agree upon such increase in price as may be found justified in the circumstances.

5. In order to carry out the objective of facilitating and stimulating the maximum possible production of rubber, Brazil agrees:

a) To make available funds of the Government of Brazil in the amount of CR ten million dollars (local currency) for the purpose of facilitating and stimulating the maximum production of rubber, including specifically the purpose of providing an incentive for placing imported labor on the sergingas (rubber tappers) and encouraging the opening of new estradas (highways). The above fund shall be increased by the amount of any fortuitous profit arising by reason of any difference between the prices received by the Banco de Crédito da Borracha for rubber on hand at the commencement of the premium period.

b) To take such action as may be necessary to assure that the producers, merchants and others engaged in the production and handling of rubber in Brazil will receive their proportionate part of the full thirty-three and a third percent premium hereinabove mentioned.

c) To take such action as may be necessary to assure that the taxes on rubber imposed by the producing states shall not be applicable to the premium of thirty-three and a third percent hereinabove mentioned, and that existing federal and state taxes on rubber will not be increased nor new taxes imposed while the said premium is being paid.

d) To take action as may be necessary to assure the effectuation of the practical measures already agreed upon by the Commission for the Control of the Washington Accords and RDC in furtherance of the rubber program insofar as much measures are not inconsistent with the provisions of this agreement.

e) To take such steps as may be necessary to bring about the establishment of the most favorable rate of exchange as applying to all exchange required for the RDC expenditures in Brazil, except for the purchase of rubber.

It is understood that this note, together with your acceptance thereof, shall constitute an agreement between the parties to be formalized by the exchange of notes between the appropriate Brazilian and American authorities in Brazil.[11]

With assurances of my highest regards, I remain,

Very sincerely,
D.H. Allen President

HULL

• • • • •

102.8951 Rio de Janeiro: Airgram
The Secretary of State to the Ambassador in Brazil (Caffery)[12]
Washington, 29 January 1944, 1900 Hours

A-113. For McAshan from Allen RDC. Following is acceptance letter of the Commission for Control of the Washington Accords dated 26 January signed by Dr Boucas;
"Dear Mr Allen: This serves to acknowledge your letter of today's date[13] conveying in its five points and addenda, the conditions agreed between us for payment up to 31 March 1945, of the premium of thirty-three and a third percent on the "Fixed price" in force, as set forth in our agreement on rubber.

The various items of your communication cover all the points which have been under discussion since the 6th instant, and, merely as a matter of routine, I wish to confirm our understanding to the effect that the contracts between the RDC and the SNAPP will continue to be in force except as to the part modified by No. 3 of item 2 (page 3).

I take this opportunity to express again to you and to the entire Board of the RDC the warmest appreciation on our part of the spirit of cooperation which has ever governed our relationship since 1942 and which has not once again been confirmed, constituting, without any doubt, a most effective and valuable contribution to the policy of good neighborliness.

Your letter of 26 January, in conjunction with this letter to you, constitutes a final agreement between us, which contents I am transmitting in due form to the Minister of Finance, President of our Commission in Rio de Janeiro, and which as stated in your letter is to be formalized by the exchange of notes between the appropriate Brazilian and American authorities in Brazil.

With the renewed expression of my highest consideration, I remain.

Sincerely yours,

V.F. Boucas
Executive Director,
(Allen)

HULL

The preceding exchange between the governments of Brazil and US dated 28 January 1944, marked the beginning a reduction in US participation in the rubber project in the Amazon. The US is continuing to buy all of the rubber possible at an increased price of thirty-three and a third percent raising the price of Acre-fina to sixty cents per pound. But, they were no longer obligated to the various tenants of the original accords dated 3 March 1942, wherein they were involved in providing transportation and logistical support for the rubber tappers and those involved in building the new structure of the rubber project.

"The RDC also decided to end its program to supply food, fuel and basic supplies at cost for Amazonian rubber producers, leaving the supply side of the rubber trade to the aviadores. The RDC claimed to have already spent more than its entire five million budgets allocated under the Washington Accords to increase rubber production. For its part, the Brazilian government pledged almost a half million dollars to support increased rubber production."[14]

• • • • •

102.8951 Rio de Janeiro
The Secretary of State to the Ambassador in Brazil (Caffery)[15]
Washington, 4 February 1944, 2200 Hours

391. It is suggested that the agreement for a price premium be utilized by you for insisting that immediate steps be taken by the Banco de Borracha to establish in northeast Brazil (and especially Natal, Maceio, Recife and Bahia) an adequate purchasing policy and price in order that rubber producers in that region will be able to find a ready market at a price that is profitable and in order at the same time to encourage those merchants who deal customarily in rubber to renew their interest in purchasing and collecting it in the interior to be sold to the Rubber Credit Bank subsequently. The lack of organization in this area by the Bank has been emphasized, as you know, by recent reports of technicians, merchants and producers are completely discouraged by this lack. Fleischman has also confirmed this fact here in person. This matter will be brought to Boucas attention by me.

Foregoing is from Allen for McAshan Rubber Development.

Hull

• • • • •

The Government of Brazil[16] undertakes to permit the importation into Brazil of synthetic rubber and other plastics having similar properties and utilization duty free, and to permit the use thereof in national industry to the extent necessary to effectuate the purposes of this agreement.

The Government of Brazil undertakes to bring about, as rapidly as may be found feasible, the maximum practicable reduction in the consumption of natural crude rubber within Brazil below the quote of eight thousand five hundred tons per year already established and to encourage the maximum practicable utilization of reclaimed rubber, synthetic rubber and similar plastics.

As a step in the application of this policy, the Government of Brazil undertakes to bring about, as rapidly as may be found practicable, the adoption by all tire and tube manufacturers within Brazil of the types of tire construction known in the US as S-5 or S-7, each of which contemplates the use of about thirty-five percent of synthetic rubber or similar plastics in place of natural crude rubber.

RDC agrees to such increase in the overall consumption quote of ten thousand tons established in the agreement of 3 October 1942, as may result from (a) unrestricted use of reclaimed rubber and (b) the use of synthetic rubber and similar plastics in accordance with the plan and arrangement herein agreed upon; it being estimated that this will enable the Brazilian rubber manufacturing industry to operate at maximum capacity.

The above arrangement is to be formalized in Rio de Janeiro and would, I believe, require the approval of President Vargas since it alters a previous decree.

As a result of discussions with technicians of Goodyear, Firestone, and the Rubber Director's Office and Boucas; it has been agreed that the quickest and most effective way of enabling the utilization of synthetic rubber in Brazil is to have the technicians of the four tire manufacturing companies in Brazil plus two technicians from manufacturers of miscellaneous rubber goods, preferably Orion[17] and one other proceed to the US as promptly as possible accompanied by Dr Maffei or such other representative as may be designated by the Government of Brazil to spend one month in the US visiting tire factories and studying the utilization of synthetic in the US. We have agreed to pay the transportation of the members of this mission other than Firestone and Goodyear to the US and within the US while on official business plus such per diem as we may be legally permitted to pay. We will advise later with respect to the rate of per diem.

It is intended that upon the return of this Mission to Brazil the mission would be constituted a technical committee to provide required technical information and to assist rubber manufacturers in the utilization of synthetic. Copies of the documents concerned are being forwarded to by airmail.[18]

We have also agreed to extend the price premium of thirty-three and a third for a further period of one year, i.e. until 31 March 1946, in order to aid the producers of natural rubber during the 1945 season. We will advise later when this information may be made public. We have likewise agreed to extend to 31 December 1944, the period during which the remainder of the sixteen thousand laborers may be recruited, delivered to the Amazon and transported up river to CAETA under the agreement between RDC and the Government of Brazil dated 6 September 1943.[19] Boucas plans to arrive Rio about 15 August.

Although Boucas and Sousa Costa have agreed to the foregoing, we have not yet received their written confirmation. (Allen)

Stettinius

In the above agreement, we see for the first time the mention of synthetic rubber and the request by the US that Brazil accept duty free synthetic rubber to augment their rubber stocks so that they would be able to export more natural rubber to the US. The recommended mix of synthetic was about thirty-five percent. In order to facilitate this new program, the US agreed to pay the transportation and per diem expenses for one month for all participants, with the exception of employees of Goodyear and Firestone.

• • • • •

832.6176/8-44: Airgram
Rio de Janeiro, 9 August 1944, 1130 Hours
(Received 21 August, 0800 Hours)

A-1493. Following the receipt of Department's A-1045, 31 July 1400 hours, "For Neumann from Allen, RDC," my Economic Counselor[20] discussed the contents of the airgram with officials of the Rio de Janeiro office of RDC and with Mr Utz of the Washington office of RDC, who is now visiting Brazil.

My Economic Counselor expressed surprise that RDC in Washington had not consulted the Embassy on the understandings reached in Washington with Senhor Valentim Boucas. He added that if the views of the Embassy had been requested, the Embassy would have recommended that the extension of the price premium of thirty-three and a third percent on crude rubber be withheld pending the signing and promulgation of the decree-law on synthetic rubber and other plastics. The local officials of the RDC were under the impression that the decree-law and the price premium were tied together, but in view of the Department's telegram 2365 of 1 August, 2200 hours ("From RDC Allen to Newmann"), authorizing public announcement of the extension of the premium payment, they said that they would check this point with their officials in Washington.

They subsequently reported that there was no connection between the two matters and that the RDC had informed other rubber producing countries in the Americas of the extension of the premium.

In reply to the Embassy's question as to whether or not they had any problems outstanding with the Commission to Control the Washington

Agreements, which administers the rubber agreements in Brazil, they said that the Brazilian Government has not yet put into effect the development fund of ten millions Cruzeiros as provided for in the agreement of 8 February 1944, and that other matters were still pending. The Embassy representative remarked that, in the opinion of the Embassy, the extension of the price premium should have been used as bargaining power to obtain prompt promulgation of the decree-law on synthetic rubber and other plastics and prompt settlement of all important matters pending with the Commission to Control the Washington Agreements. He stated that a public announcement at this time extending the price premium until 31 March 1946 and, might prejudice the overall program for the procurement of strategic materials because producers and exporters of the materials would use it as a basis for requesting an increase in process for their produce. He added that the development would be untimely and unfortunately, in view of the fact that the Brazilian Government recently increased the export prices on tantalite and beryl and which the Embassy and the USCC succeeded in having postponed but only after long and difficult negotiations.

The Embassy hopes that the Brazilian Government will not delay in promulgating the legislation necessary to implement the aforementioned agreement on synthetic rubber and other plastics, but desires to point out that in as much as the RDC has decided to announce the extension of the price premium at this time and not tie it in with the synthetic rubber plan, the Embassy and the RDC here will be deprived of a strong bargaining weapon.

The airgram under reference states that the arrangement on synthetic rubber will be formalized in Rio de Janeiro. The Embassy assumes that this meant that it will take the form of an exchange of notes between the Embassy and the Foreign office. If this is correct, the Embassy suggests that the Foreign office should have been consulted concerning the terms of the proposed arrangement, even though the provisions are favorable to Brazil.

Caffery

• • • • •

832.616/7-3144: Telegram
The Secretary of State to the Ambassador in Brazil (Caffery)

Chapter 14: The High Price of Rubber

Washington, 13 September 1944, 1825 Hours

A-1248. For Neumann from Allen RDC. Referring to the telephone conversation, we confirm that we are now prepared to consider an extension of the price, premium to 31 December 1946. The agreed extension to 31 March 1946 is intended to cover rubber produced in the 1945 season in the same manner that the initial premium was designed to cover rubber produced in the 1944 season. The governments of countries concerned other than Brazil, have been advised of the extension to 31 March 1946, and have accepted such extension and have made public announcement thereof.

As regards profits of the Banco da Borracha, our understanding is as follows:

That profits derived from the application of the price premium to stocks of rubber on hand as of 9 February 1944, the sale of salvage rubber and volume premiums, are all to be paid into a special development fund to be used for the benefit of the rubber program.

That five percent of annual net profits shall be paid into a reserve fund until the said fund equals twenty percent of the capital of the Bank.

The dividends are to be limited to twelve percent of the capital of the Bank and that any excess is to be paid into the development (of the bank).

We understand that the CCWA is informally inquiring whether we would be willing to consider limiting dividends to six percent instead of twelve percent if the Government of Brazil would likewise agree. We do not perceive any objection to this proposal but official approval on our part would require action by the Directors.

We would suggest you look into the question of whether the five percent reserve for losses on loans is adequate and, if not, whether it might not be preferable to add to such reserve profits in excess of six percent at least until the full twenty percent reserve has been achieved.

In connection with the utilization of the development fund, we wish to emphasize that our primary interest lies in the measures designed to bring about immediate stimulation of rubber production rather than in long-term plantation projects. The language of the applicable agreements seems to indicate that the fund was intended to be used for such immediate stimulation rather than long-term projects but it may not be wise to oppose the use of any part of the fund for such long-term projects, particularly in view of President Vargas' interest in such projects. (Allen)

Hull

• • • • •

832.24/11344: Telegram
The Acting Secretary of State to the Charge in Brazil (Donnelly)
Washington, 3 November 1944, 1300 Hours

3321. Department understands from RDC that one factor possibly delaying issuance of Brazilian decree concerning use of synthetic rubber is a doubt regarding the essentiality of natural rubber in the United Nations war effort.

The Combined Raw Materials Board is preparing a release, which in substance will reiterate that the vital need for natural rubber is as great today as it has ever been during the course of the war. This arises from the continued necessity to use natural rubber in greater or less quantities in a wide range of products, particularly large size and heavy-duty aircraft, military and truck-size tires for which the direct military demand continues to exceed supply. In addition, the movement of raw materials and finished products and working to and from factories creates large demands for the heavy duty tires for trucking and bus operations.

The Department therefore endorses the statement that the need for every pound of natural rubber that can be obtained is critical.

Please inform the RDC representative. And so advise the Brazilian Foreign Office if you perceive no …

• • • • •

800.554/2-144
The Charge in Bazil (Donnelly) to Secretary of State
No. 18958
Rio de Janeiro, 1 December 1944.
(Received 7 December)

Sir, I have the honor to refer to the Embassy's telegram No. 4222 of 27 November 1944, reporting the approval by President Vargas of the synthetic rubber agreement, and to previous correspondence relating to the progress of the negotiations on this subject.

In the course of the consideration of the agreement for the use by the Brazilian rubber industry of the synthetic product, a number of objections had to be overcome. The Ministry of Foreign Affairs proposed several alterations, the principal one designed to reduce the consumption of crude rubber to seven hundred ton, which would have had the effect to negating the entire purpose of the agreement. Through representations made by the Embassy and the RDC, the Ministry of Foreign Affairs was persuaded to withdraw the proposal. The agreement was then approved by the Ministry of Finance and forwarded to the President.

The Embassy followed the matter closely and was able to expedite the approval of the agreement by the President in its final form early this week.

Respectfully yours,

WALTER J. DONNELY

• • • • •

800.554/12-144
The Charge in Brazil (Donnelly) to the Secretary of State
No. 189058
Rio de Janeiro, 1 December 1944.
(Received 5 January 1945)

Sir, I have the honor to refer to previous correspondence concerning the agreement for the use of synthetic rubber by the Brazilian rubber industries and now to transmit copies of an exchange of notes between this Embassy and the Ministry of Foreign Affairs of Brazil formally recognizing the provisions of the agreement reached between the RDC and the Commission for the Control of the Washington Agreements.

Although the Decree-Law implementing this agreement has not yet been signed it is understood to be now in the office of the President and it is likely that it will be promulgated within the week.

Respectfully yours,

For the Charge d'Affaires a.i.; Harold S. Tewell
First Secretary of the Embassy

• • • • •

The American Charge in Brazil (Donnelly) to the Brazilian Acting Minister for Foreign Affairs (Leao Velloso)
Rio de Janeiro, 22 December 1944
No. 2352

Excellency: I have the honor to inform Your Excellency that my Government agrees to the provisions of your note of this date and considers the agreement completed by the exchange of these notes in accordance with the following terms:

The Government of the United States of America, having in mind the agreements signed between our two Governments on 3 March and 3 October 1942, referring respectively to natural rubber and manufactured rubber, and considering that in the present emergency natural rubber continues to be of great necessity to the war and civilian industry of the United Nations, and desiring, on the other hand to emphasize the mutual spirit of cooperation and assistance which has prevailed in the solution of problems related to such strategic materials as rubber, agrees to the following modifications in the above mentioned agreement of 3 October 1942, in accordance with the decision reached between the Commissão de Controle dos Acordos de Washington and the RDC, successor to the Rubber Reserve Company.

I: The Government of Brazil undertakes to permit the importation from the United States of America of synthetic rubber, and other plastics having similar properties and utilization, free of any other custom duties and other thereto, social security taxes, and of any other clearance fees or charges, and to allow the use thereof in the national industry, in the proportion necessary to carry out the terms of the present agreement, without altering the fiscal regime which grants to the rubber products factories exemption of duties for the importation of other raw materials utilized by them.

II: The Government of Brazil undertakes to bring about, as soon as possible, the maximum practicable reduction in the consumption of natural crude rubber in the country below the present annual quota of eight thousand, five hundred tons, and to promote to the maximum use of reclaimed rubber as well as of synthetic rubber, and other plastics of a similar nature.

III: For the purpose of carrying out such understandings, the Government of Brazil undertakes to establish as soon as possible the adoption by the manufacturers of tires and tubes of the manufacturing methods employed in the US, known as the S-5 or S-7 in which there are used about thirty-five percent of synthetic rubber, or other plastics of a similar nature in substitution of natural crude rubber. The technical data necessary for the adoption of the above-mentioned processes shall be furnished free of charge by the RDC to the Brazilian rubber goods industry through the Commission de Contrôle dos Acordos de Washington.

IV: The Government of Brazil undertakes to prevent the re-exportation of any quantity of synthetic and of any other plastics of a similar nature supplied to Brazil by the United States of America, through the intermediation of the RDC, by virtue of the present agreement, unless such plastics shall have been transformed into manufactured goods, in conformity with the provisions of the 3 October 1942 agreement between Brazil and the United States of America.

V: RDC undertakes to supply to Brazil such quantity of synthetic rubber, or other plastics of a similar nature, as may be necessary to carry out the terms of the present agreement, which quantity may not be less than 2,500 tons per year, at the following export prices f.o.b. factory in the United States of America:

GR-S (Buna S): US$0.36 (thirty-six cents) per lb

GR-S (Special): US$0.3 (thirty-six cents) per lb

GR-M (Neoprene): US$0.45 (forty-five cents) per lb.

The basic prices above set forth may be reduced, in which case the RDC shall enter into agreement with the Commissão de Contrôle dos Acordos de Washington in order to set up a new price schedule.

VI: RDC, in addition to the tires and tubes that it is obligated to purchase, in accordance with the provisions of the 3 October 1942 agreement agrees to buy, during the period established by the present agreement and in conformity with the terms and provisions of the 3 October 1942, such additional quantities of tires and tubes as may become available for exportation and which may have been produced by virtue of the use of synthetic rubber, or of other plastics of a similar nature, in the industry of said products.

VII: RDC agrees with the increase of the total consumption quote of ten thousand tons per year, established by the 3 October 1942 agreement, which may result from:

— unlimited use of reclaimed rubber

— use of synthetic rubber, or other plastics of a similar nature, in conformity with the plan and arrangement hereby established, it being estimated that by carrying out the above measures the production capacity of the Brazilian rubber product industry will increase to the maximum; it being also understood that all of the tires and tubes manufactures in Brazil, during the period specified in the present agreement, in excess of the essential necessities of the country, figured in accordance with the 3 October 1942 agreements as not being more than seven thousand five hundred tons shall be sold to the United States of America, in accordance with the provisions of the above mentioned agreement of 3 October 1942.

VIII: In order to render, the most efficient and practicable technical assistance in connection with the use of synthetic rubber, the RDC undertakes, upon understanding with the …

• • • • •

832.654/12-2644
The Charge in Brazil (Donnelly) to thee Secretary of State
No. 19294
Rio de Janeiro, 26 December 1944
(Received 5 January 1945)

Sir, I have the honor to refer to previous correspondence concerning the agreement for the use of synthetic rubber by the Brazilian rubber industries and not to transmit copies of an exchange of notes between this Embassy and his Ministry of Foreign Affairs of Brazil formally recognizing the provisions of the agreement reached between the RDC and the Commission for the Control of the Washington Agreements.

Although the Decree-Law implementing this agreement has not yet been signed, it is understood to be now in the office of the President and it is likely that it will be promulgated within the week.

Respectfully yours,

For the Charge d' Affaires a.i.; Harold S. Tewell
First Secretary of Embassy

CHAPTER 15
WAR ENDS

By 1943, North Africa had been secured by the Allied forces. With this victory the German U-boat threat in the South Atlantic came to an end. Royal Navy and United States (US) Navy merchant ships were able to move without difficulties through the South Atlantic, but more important, Brazilian merchant ships could once again move freely from southern Brazil up the coast and into the Amazon basin without German U-boat threats. The US continued to extensively utilize the air bases along Brazil's northern coast, but once the Allied Forces controlled North Africa, these bases had a less critical role.

Not unlike what happened in the war of the Pacific at the end of World War II, as soon as the war ended, the Americans left the Amazon and Brazil almost immediately. There were those that thought that the agreements between US and Brazil at the outset of the war would assure that the US would lay claim to the Amazon basin and possibly more. Nothing could have been further from the truth. Abandoned tractors in the middle of the forest, unfinished ships in the shipyards, construction structures left behind on the banks of the rivers, and airports handed over to the astonished Brazilian workers. The Americans had retreated.

After the Japanese surrender in August of 1945, Brazilian rubber was no longer of interest. To compound the problem, Brazil's rubber production never reached the anticipated tonnage of thirty-five thousand to five hundred thousand tons per year. In 1943, Brazil produced twenty-two thousand seven hundred thirty-five tons of rubber of which only ten thousand nine hundred thirty-one tons were exported to the US. Brazil reserved the remaining eleven thousand eight hundred four tons for domestic consumption.[1] Utensils, machines, trucks, tractors, ships, boat's radio equipment, the Rubber Development Corporation (RDC) sold everything to the Brazilian Credit Bank of rubber at cut-rate prices.

In the interest of propaganda, there was an official ceremony here and there. American workers transmitted recognition to the vital role the Brazilians played in the war effort. A hospital built and operated by the US-RDC during the war in Manaus was transferred to the Brazilian government. In addition to all this, Henry Ford announced the end of the attempts to ration latex in the country. He gave up on the properties of Fordlândia and Belterra, on the banks of the Tapajós in Pará.

The main problem after the war ended was the price of rubber. Earlier there was the concern that the defeated Japanese would introduce the South American rubber blight into the Asian rubber plantations. When this did not materialize, once again, cheap Asian rubber became readily available, and this rubber and synthetic rubber flooded the international market with prices three times lower than Brazilian latex. And once again, the bottom fell out of the Brazilian economy. Brazil met at the National Rubber Conference to decide what to do. The main problem was the price of rubber, which could guarantee survival against the competition, and this was no longer a possibility.

With the demobilization of American troops and the end of Getúlio Vargas's dictatorship the Brazilian Government faced the problem of thousands of men still in the jungle cutting the rubber trees and another nineteen thousand dependents, and the plight of the rubber soldiers. In an editorial column "The Tragedy of the Rubber Soldiers," in the *Jornal do Brasil* of Rio de Janeiro that spitefully accuses: "false promises, reign of lies, reckless fantasy, a battle without glory." The newspapers stated, "twenty-three thousand people rotted in the mud, with no bread, no medical assistance or medicine to treat their intense fevers, the lack of vitamins, the assault of parasites." A chronicle of Ruben Braga, reprinted in the newspaper *O Acre*, denounced, "the levity that put into play thousands of Brazilian lives, poor devils, sacrificed in a fight of vanity, ambitions and politics."

On 28 April 1948, there was a final report from the Rubber Development Division of the US government stating that between April 1942 and 30 June 1947, the US paid $1,041,161,099.45 for foreign rubber purchased for the World War II effort. Of that amount, $40,081,328.65 was paid to Brazil for rubber from the Amazon. This report was signed by A.J. Hildrather, Assistant Chief. The following is a copy of that report. This was, in addition to the $100,000,000.00 line of credit provided to Brazil to set up the rubber extraction program plus the $5,000,000.00 advance for the improvement of sanitation and infrastructural needs in the rubber estates. All of this was in the March 3,1942 accord between Brazil and the United States.

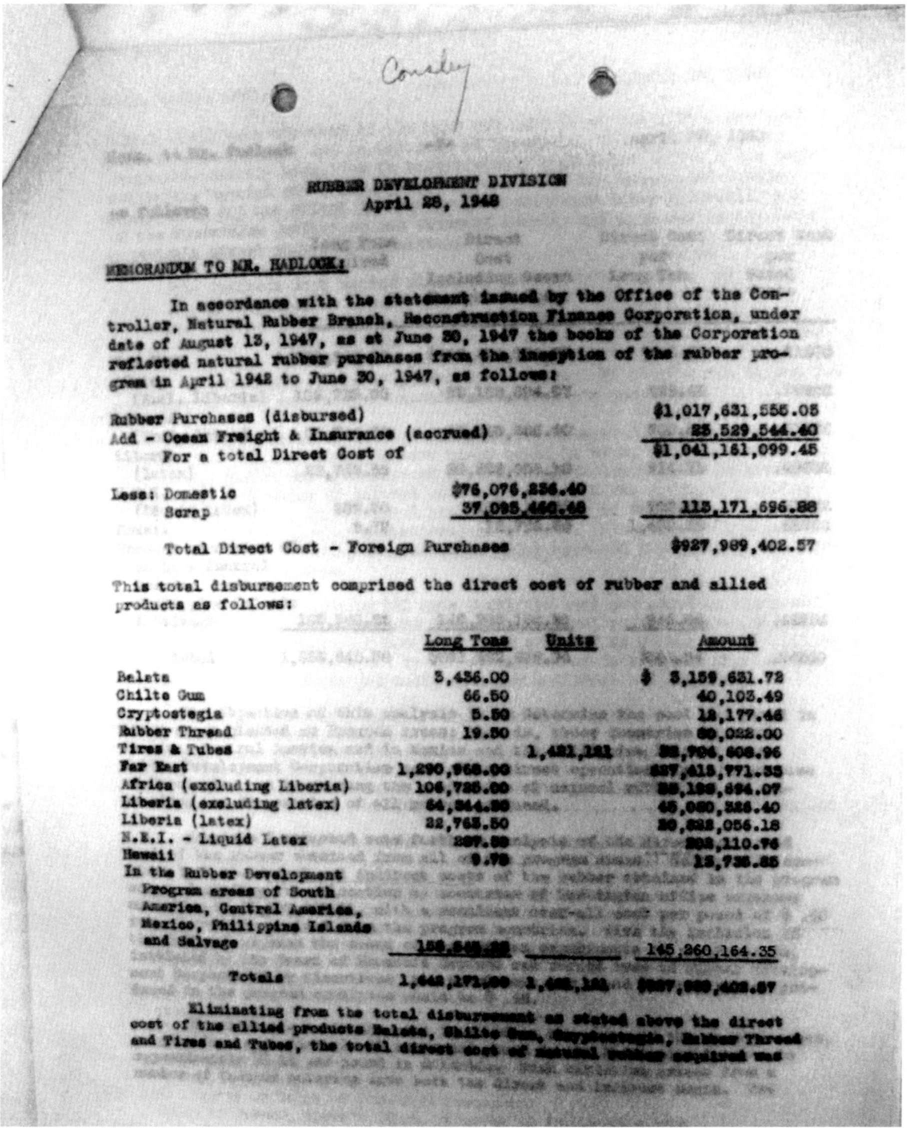

RUBBER DEVELOPMENT DIVISION
April 28, 1948

MEMORANDUM TO MR. HADLOCK:

In accordance with the statement issued by the Office of the Controller, Natural Rubber Branch, Reconstruction Finance Corporation, under date of August 13, 1947, as at June 30, 1947 the books of the Corporation reflected natural rubber purchases from the inception of the rubber program in April 1942 to June 30, 1947, as follows:

Rubber Purchases (disbursed)		$1,017,631,555.05
Add - Ocean Freight & Insurance (accrued)		23,529,544.40
For a total Direct Cost of		$1,041,161,099.45
Less: Domestic	$76,076,236.40	
Scrap	37,095,460.48	113,171,696.88
Total Direct Cost - Foreign Purchases		$927,989,402.57

This total disbursement comprised the direct cost of rubber and allied products as follows:

	Long Tons	Units	Amount
Balata	3,436.00		$ 3,159,631.72
Chilte Gum	66.50		40,103.49
Cryptostegia	5.50		12,177.46
Rubber Thread	19.50		80,022.00
Tires & Tubes		1,421,121	[illegible],706,608.96
Far East	1,290,968.00		827,418,771.35
Africa (excluding Liberia)	106,725.00		85,198,894.07
Liberia (excluding latex)	64,344.50		45,080,326.40
Liberia (latex)	22,763.50		20,828,056.18
N.E.I. - Liquid Latex	287.50		208,110.76
Hawaii	9.78		13,736.85
In the Rubber Development Program areas of South America, Central America, Mexico, Philippine Islands and Salvage	[illegible]		145,260,164.35
Totals	1,642,171.00	[illegible]	$927,989,402.57

Eliminating from the total disbursement as stated above the direct cost of the allied products Balata, Chilte Gum, Cryptostegia, Rubber Thread and Tires and Tubes, the total direct cost of natural rubber acquired was

Memo. to Mr. Hadlock -2- April 28, 1948

as follows:

	Long Tons Acquired	Direct Cost Including Ocean Freight & Ins. Accrued	Direct Cost per Long Ton	Direct Cost per Pound Cents
Far East	1,290,968.00	$627,415,771.33	$486.00	.21696
Africa (Excl. Liberia)	106,725.00	53,198,694.07	498.46	.22252
Liberia (Excl. latex)	64,344.50	45,080,326.40	700.60	.31276
Liberia (latex)	22,763.50	20,822,056.18	914.71	.40835
N.E.I. (Liquid Latex)	287.50	202,110.76	702.99	.31383
Hawaii	9.75	13,735.85	1,408.80	.62892
Program countries of South & Central America, Mexico, Philippine Islands & Salvage	153,545.25	145,260,164.35	946.04	.42234
Total	1,638,643.50	$891,992,858.94	$544.34	.24300

The objective of this analysis is to determine the cost per pound in those areas classed as Program Areas; that is, those countries in South America, Central America and in Mexico and the Philippine Islands where Rubber Development Corporation carried on direct operations for the purpose of developing and increasing the production of natural rubber and of controlling the disposition of all rubber produced.

Schedule I attached sets forth an analysis of the direct per pound cost of the rubber obtained from all of the program areas. Schedule II combined both the direct and indirect costs of the rubber obtained in the program areas, including the allocation by countries of Washington office expenses amounting to $9,390,258.91, with a resultant over-all cost per pound of $ .60 for all rubber obtained from the program countries. With the inclusion in the indirect expense the costs of the Haitian experiments on cryptostegia, initiated by the Board of Economic Warfare and turned over to Rubber Development Corporation by directives, the total cost per pound for all rubber produced in the program countries would be $ .68.

Considerable variation will be noted in the costs in the several areas, ranging from approximately 27 cents per pound in the Philippine Islands to approximately $1.14 per pound in Colombia. Such variation arises from a number of factors entering into both the direct and indirect costs. The

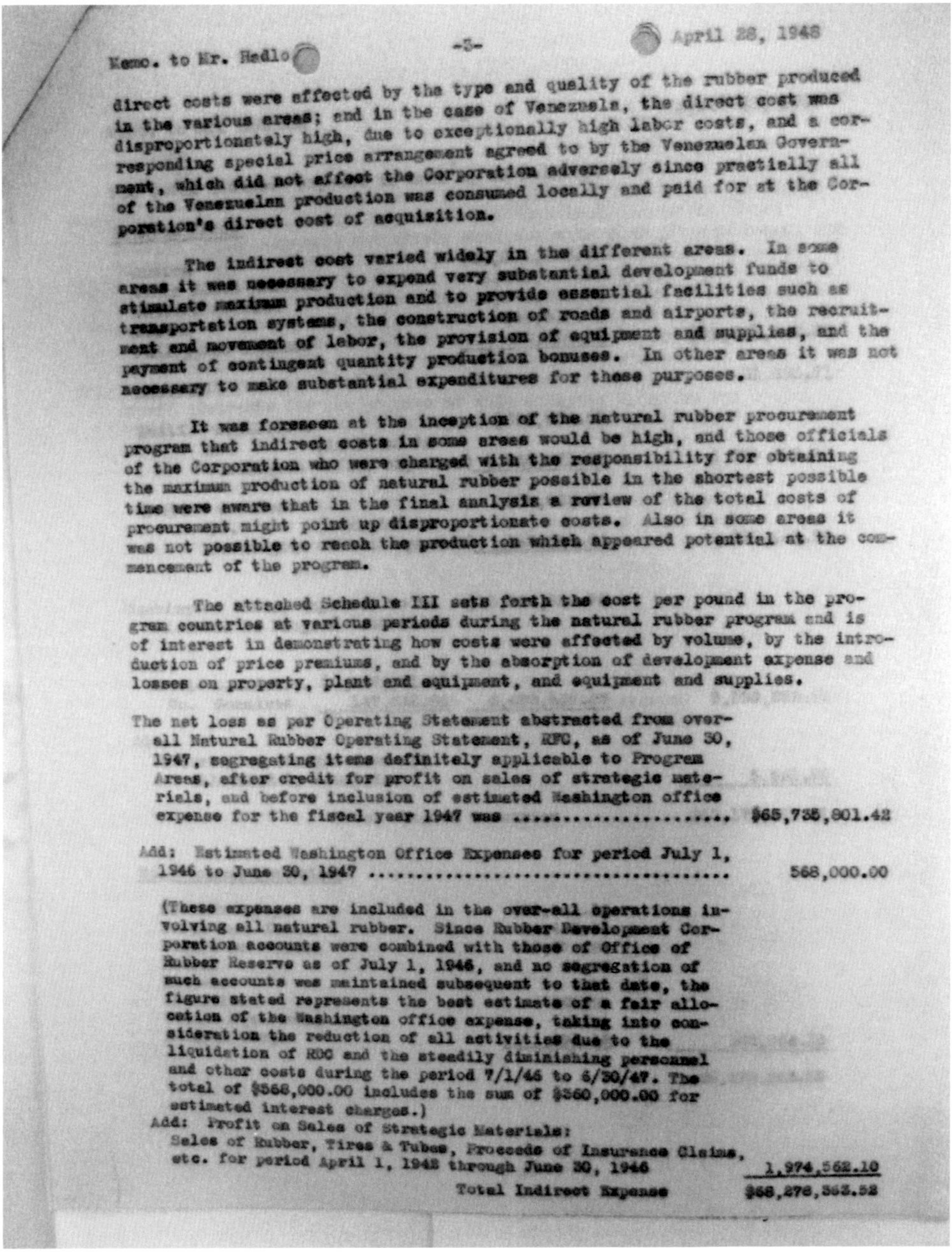

Memo. to Mr. Hedlo -3- April 28, 1948

direct costs were affected by the type and quality of the rubber produced in the various areas; and in the case of Venezuela, the direct cost was disproportionately high, due to exceptionally high labor costs, and a corresponding special price arrangement agreed to by the Venezuelan Government, which did not affect the Corporation adversely since practically all of the Venezuelan production was consumed locally and paid for at the Corporation's direct cost of acquisition.

The indirect cost varied widely in the different areas. In some areas it was necessary to expend very substantial development funds to stimulate maximum production and to provide essential facilities such as transportation systems, the construction of roads and airports, the recruitment and movement of labor, the provision of equipment and supplies, and the payment of contingent quantity production bonuses. In other areas it was not necessary to make substantial expenditures for these purposes.

It was foreseen at the inception of the natural rubber procurement program that indirect costs in some areas would be high, and those officials of the Corporation who were charged with the responsibility for obtaining the maximum production of natural rubber possible in the shortest possible time were aware that in the final analysis a review of the total costs of procurement might point up disproportionate costs. Also in some areas it was not possible to reach the production which appeared potential at the commencement of the program.

The attached Schedule III sets forth the cost per pound in the program countries at various periods during the natural rubber program and is of interest in demonstrating how costs were affected by volume, by the introduction of price premiums, and by the absorption of development expense and losses on property, plant and equipment, and equipment and supplies.

The net loss as per Operating Statement abstracted from over-all Natural Rubber Operating Statement, RFC, as of June 30, 1947, segregating items definitely applicable to Program Areas, after credit for profit on sales of strategic materials, and before inclusion of estimated Washington office expense for the fiscal year 1947 was	$65,735,801.42
Add: Estimated Washington Office Expenses for period July 1, 1946 to June 30, 1947	568,000.00
(These expenses are included in the over-all operations involving all natural rubber. Since Rubber Development Corporation accounts were combined with those of Office of Rubber Reserve as of July 1, 1946, and no segregation of such accounts was maintained subsequent to that date, the figure stated represents the best estimate of a fair allocation of the Washington office expense, taking into consideration the reduction of all activities due to the liquidation of RDC and the steadily diminishing personnel and other costs during the period 7/1/46 to 6/30/47. The total of $568,000.00 includes the sum of $360,000.00 for estimated interest charges.)	
Add: Profit on Sales of Strategic Materials: Sales of Rubber, Tires & Tubes, Proceeds of Insurance Claims, etc. for period April 1, 1942 through June 30, 1946	1,974,562.10
Total Indirect Expense	$68,278,363.52

Memo. to Mr. Hadlock -4- April 28, 1948

The total indirect expense is made up as follows:

Program Areas

Amazon		$40,081,328.65	
Other South America		6,439,360.08	
Central America		4,240,826.94	
Mexico		966,409.33	
Philippine Islands		93,524.83	$51,821,449.83
Liberia			31,483.71
Haiti - S.H.A.D.A.		$379,594.01	
Do. (included in Washington office expenses)		6,346,021.03	6,725,615.04
Haiti - Gonaives		$50,883.08	
Do. (included in Washington office expenses)		147,546.84	198,429.92
Washington Office Expenses to be allocated to Program Countries		$15,883,826.78	
Less:			
Haiti- S.H.A.D.A.	$6,346,021.03		
Do. Gonaives	147,546.84	6,493,567.87	9,390,258.91
Add:			
Unidentified charges from RFC not allocated by countries			6,561.96
Total Program Countries			$68,173,799.37

Non-Program Countries

British Malaya	$56,904.18	
Dutch East Indies	24,625.14	
French Indo-China	22,372.30	
Hawaii	22.27	
Batavia	4.91	
Australia	327.30	
French Equatorial Africa	16.91	
Belgian Congo	291.14	104,564.15
		$68,278,363.52

Memo. to Mr. Hadlock -5- April 28, 1948

In the attached Schedule II it will be noted that in arriving at the total of direct and indirect costs applied to the rubber purchased in the program areas $51,821,449.83 has been included as the total foreign office expenses definitely chargeable to such program areas, and $9,390,256.91 of Washington office expense has been allocated to the various countries falling within the program areas. If a portion of this latter amount were to be allocated to the procurement of natural rubber from the Far East, Africa and other sources, it is apparent that the total per pound cost of the rubber obtained from the program countries would be correspondingly reduced. However, since there appears to be no sound formula by which such allocation can be made, it has been deemed advisable for the purpose of this analysis to allow the entire total of the Washington office expenses to be applied to the program areas.

The total indirect expenses used in this analysis includes a Reserve for Valuation of Assets as of June 30, 1947 of $6,223,476.00, and any recoveries in excess of the amount reserved would produce a corresponding reduction in the total per pound cost of the rubber procured.

A. J. Hildreth
A. J. Hildreth
Assistant Chief

Attachments-3

• • • • •

Mr William E. Simons,
125 East Elder Street,
South Bend, Indiana
24 November 1947
State Department
Washington DC

Gentlemen,
Coming directly to the point, I want to know if the following statement made by the pastor of the Grace Methodist Church of this city. I am a member of this church and am a Democrat. He is a Republican, as a large percent of the Methodist Ministers are here in the North.

Here is the statement made from the pulpit:

"Before the close of World War II the Government sponsored the sending of eighteen thousand men to the rubber plantations in South America to work for the big rubber companies. SEVENTEEN THOUSAND OF THIS number DIED without medical attention and nothing was said about it."

WAS such an expedition ever sent?

If so, who by and under what authority?

What is the truth about his statement?

I have talked with several members of the church and some high up officials and I say to you they all declare it is not true.

I beg to ask you to give me information and thank you most sincerely for it.

Yours truly, (signed)

Walter E. Simons

Chapter 15: War Ends

• • • • •

Rubber Development Division
22 December 1947
Mr William E. Simons,
125 East Elder Street,
South Bend, Indiana

Dear Mr Simons,
Reference is made to your letter of 18 November 1947, addressed to the Department of State, with regard to rubber tappers in South America, which letter has been referred to this office for reply.

The statement made by the pastor of the Grace Methodist Church of your city could be interpreted to mean that this government sent eighteen thousand men to the rubber plantations in South America, which is not correct.

RDC, an instrumentality of the US government, extended financial and technical assistance to the government of several South American countries in the interest of procuring natural rubber for wartime needs. The government did not participate in the handling of the rubber laborers, nor were any such laborers sent from the US into the rubber territories of South America. The actual labor of procuring natural rubber during the war time rubber programs was performed by nationals of the countries of South America under the sponsorship and supervision of the governments of the respective countries.

The statement made by the pastor of your church probably refers to a large-scale movement of Brazilian laborers undertaken by SENTA and Brazilian agency Superintendência de Abastecimento do Vale Amazônico (SAVA), two agencies of the Brazilian government. RDC rendered financial assistance to both SENTA and SAVA to enable those agencies of the Brazilian government to provide transportation, food, lodging, minimum pay, sanitation, medical inspection and aid for laborers who were recruited from drought stricken areas of Brazil for tapping rubber trees in the Amazon Valley. The responsibility of RDC was limited entirely to rendering financial aid to these projects, which were completely under the control and direction of the Brazilian government.

The Brazilian Government undertook to provide working conditions in conformity with Brazilian labor legislation and it is understood that approximately twenty thousand workers were moved into the rubber territory. The contract with a worker provided that the Brazilian Government would furnish:

Transportation, lodging, medical and sanitary care for the worker

Board, medical care, foodstuffs, education and transportation of his dependent

Religious assistance

Financial allotment for dependents

Return to point of origin if worker could not be used.

A special fund was setup by the Brazilian government for the purpose of transporting the workers and providing food, medicine and pharmaceutical care and upon termination of the project the Brazilian government understood to return these workers to their point of origin. This office is not in possession of any statistics with respect to the mortality of either those laborers who were moved out of the drought stricken area or of those who remained.

The American technicians and other personnel that were sent to South America and Central America to assist agencies of the local governments have all been returned safely to this country.

It will be noted from the foregoing that the US government, through RDC, rendered financial assistance to the government of certain South American countries for the purpose of increasing the available supplies of natural rubber from such countries but did not have the responsibility for nor did it direct any such an activities within the countries.

Very truly yours, (signed)

G.B. Hadock
Executive Director
Office of Rubber Reserve

EPILOGUE

In October of 2009, we traveled to the city of Porto Velho on the Madeira River in the Amazon basin. We were on a fact-finding trip for our book about the Madeira Mamore Railroad, which was constructed along the Madeira Mamore River from 1867 to 1913 at a cost of 10,000 lives and $30,000,000. When we were in Porto Velho we stumbled on the story of the rubber soldiers.

The story of the old railroad that inspired our book, *Tracks in the Amazon*, but we found the story of the train was also intertwined with the story of the rubber soldiers. The inspiration for this book emerged after countless interviews with survivors of the rubber army now in their nineties and beyond. The persistent question from these amazing men and women was "when will the United States pay us for our sacrifice?"

We feel this book answers this question and for the first time since WWII, provides a clear picture of the relationship between the United States and Brazil during the years of 1942–1947. It finally puts to rest the questions of "did the US pay for the rubber?" and among other things, it documents the money trail with official papers from the files of the United States Senate never before seen.

In our quest for these answers, we became very attached to these old rubber tappers and their descendants and found many hundreds of new friends in this remote area of the world.

GLOSSARY

Arigós: rugged men.
Aviadores: middle men, who would supply the rubber tappers with their food and supplies on a credit debit system and then sell the rubber to foreign companies.
Barracão: shack.
Caboclos: mixture of a northeasterner and an Amazonian Indian.
Cachaça: sugarcane rum.
CAETA: facilitated some families to travel to an assigned rubber estate.
Capoeira: an Afro-Brazilian art form that combines elements of martial arts, music and dance.
Cearenses: someone from the State of Ceará.
Cruzeiros: currency of the time.
CTA: Center of Workers of the Amazon (Centro dos Trabalhadores da Amazônia).
DIP: Department of Press and Propaganda
Favela: Brazilian slums or ghetto.
Flagelados: Itinerant workers.
Forró: a typical northeastern dance party for the single men.
Jebond knife: styled after the Asian rubber extraction knife.
Lampião: the Jesse James of the Brazilian northeast.
Legas Camponesas: Peasant Leagues.
Manáos: previous spelling for Manaus.
Mapinguari: a legendary enormous red sloth looking beast.
RDC: Rubber Development Corporation.
Rubber Reserve Company: an Agency of the United States Government.
Saudades: a deep emotional state of nostalgic longing for an absent something or someone that one loves.
SEMTA: the Brazilian Organization for the mobilization of workers of the Amazon.
Seringalistas: Rubber elite owners of the big rubber estates.
Seringueiro: rubber tapper.
SESP: Organization working to improve health of the tappers.
Sertão: hinterland of the northeast.
Sertanejo: someone living on the Sertao.
SNAPP: In 1940, the federal government intervened to end the

subsidies and created a government-owned shipping company, Serviço de Navegação e Administração dos Portos do Pará. SNAPP had fifty-two floating vessels including ocean-going ships, riverboats, tugboats, and motor boats in its 1940 inventory. Much of the fleet was antiquated, with vessels still burning wood for fuel. The Rubber Development Corporation (RDC) collaborated with SNAPP to transport the rubber soldiers and supplies to the rubber estates. The RDC helped to modernize SNAPP by supplying up-to-date ships and riverboats; providing expert mechanics, welders and electricians to train Brazilian technicians; and delivering coal and other fuel to Belém at fixed, subsidized prices.
Tapir: a pig sized furry mammal that looks like a cross between a pig and an elephant. In Portuguese, its name is Anta.

ENDNOTES

Chapter 1

1. Neeleman, Gary, and Rose Neeleman. *Tracks in the Amazon*. Forward by Wade Davis. Salt Lake City: University of Utah Press, 2012.

Chapter 2

1. Davis, Wade. *One River: Explorations and Discoveries in the Amazon Rain Forest*. New York: Touchstone, 1997.
2. Davis, Wade. *One River: Explorations and Discoveries in the Amazon Rain Forest*. New York: Touchstone, 1997.
3. Vargas, Getúlio. "Discurso Do Rio Amazonas." Arquivo Getúlio Vargas. Manaus. 10 Oct. 1940.
4. Wirth, John D. *The Politics of Brazilian Development, 1930-1954*. Stanford: University, 1970.

Morales, Lúcia Arrais. *Vai E Vem, Vira E Volta: As Rotas Dos Soldados Da Borracha*. Fortaleza, Brazil: Governo Do Estado Do Ceará, Secretaria Da Cultura E Desporto, 2002.

5. Oliveira, Nilda Nazaré Pereira., and Benedicto Heloiz Nascimento. *A Economia Da Borracha Na Amazônia Sob O Impacto Dos Acordos De Washington E Da Criação Do Banco De Crédito Da Borracha (1942-1950)*. University of São Paulo: Thesis, 2001: 98.
6. Oliveira, Nilda Nazaré Pereira., and Benedicto Heloiz Nascimento. *A Economia Da Borracha Na Amazônia Sob O Impacto Dos Acordos De Washington E Da Criação Do Banco De Crédito Da Borracha (1942-1950)*. University of São Paulo: Thesis, 2001: 109-110.
7. Oliveira, Nilda Nazaré Pereira., and Benedicto Heloiz Nascimento. *A Economia Da Borracha Na Amazônia Sob O Impacto Dos Acordos De Washington E Da Criação Do Banco De Crédito Da Borracha (1942-1950)*. University of São Paulo: Thesis, 2001.
8. Oliveira, Nilda Nazaré Pereira., and Benedicto Heloiz Nascimento. *A Economia Da Borracha Na Amazônia Sob O Impacto Dos Acordos De Washington E Da Criação Do Banco De Crédito Da Borracha (1942-1950)*. University of São Paulo: Thesis, 2001: 111-

112.

Chapter 3

1. Davis, Wade. *One River: Explorations and Discoveries in the Amazon Rain Forest*. New York: Touchstone, 1997.
2. Davis, Wade. *One River: Explorations and Discoveries in the Amazon Rain Forest*. New York: Touchstone, 1997.
3. Davis, Wade. *One River: Explorations and Discoveries in the Amazon Rain Forest*. New York: Touchstone, 1997.
4. Davis, Wade. *One River: Explorations and Discoveries in the Amazon Rain Forest*. New York: Touchstone, 1997.
5. Jackson, Joe. *The Thief at the End of the World: Rubber, Power, and the Seeds of Empire*. New York: Viking, 2008.

Chapter 4

1. Image in Creative Commons – Attribution: Bundesarchiv, DVM 10 Bild-23-63-06 / CC-BY-SA
2. Image in the Public Domain – February 2, 1940 by Ensign Richard D. Sampson, USN
3. Wilkinson, Xenia Vunovic, M.A. *Tapping the Amazon for Victory: Brazil's "Battle for Rubber" of World War II*. Diss. Georgetown University, 2009. Washington DC: Graduate School of Arts and Sciences Of Georgetown University, 2009: 2.
4. McCann, Frank D. *The Brazilian-American Alliance, 1937-1945*. Princeton: Princeton UP, 1974.

Chapter 5

1. McCann, Frank D. *The Brazilian-American Alliance, 1937-1945*. Princeton: Princeton UP, 1974: 216-220.
2. McCann, Frank D. *The Brazilian-American Alliance, 1937-1945*. Princeton: Princeton UP, 1974: 275-277.
3. Harrison, John R. *Fairwing – Brazil Tales of the South Atlantic*. Hockessin, DE: John R. Harrison, 2011: 41.
4. Harrison, John R. *Fairwing – Brazil Tales of the South Atlantic*. Hockessin, DE: John R. Harrison, 2011: 13.

5. Harrison, John R. *Fairwing – Brazil Tales of the South Atlantic.* Hockessin, DE: John R. Harrison, 2011: 161.
6. Harrison, John R. *Fairwing – Brazil Tales of the South Atlantic.* Hockessin, DE: John R. Harrison, 2011: 162.

Chapter 6

1. McCann, Frank D. *The Brazilian-American Alliance, 1937-1945.* Princeton: Princeton UP, 1974: 258-259.

Chapter 7

1. Wells, Sumner. Letter to Vice President Henry A. Wallace. 19 Mar. 1942. Memorandum.
2. National Archives Building, Washington, DC (NAB).
3. Not printed.
4. The Rubber Reserve Company was a purchasing agency of the Federal Loan Agency until February 24, 1942, on which date it was transferred to the Department of Commerce.
5. Federal Register 511.
6. International Agreements other than Treaties [57 Stat.] page 1319 Rubber Production—March 3, 1942, National Archives Building, Washington DC, (NAB).
7. International Agreements other than Treaties [57 Stat.] page 1318 , National Archive Building, Washington, DC (NAB).
8. International Agreements other than Treaties [57 Stat.] page 1321, National Archive Building, Washington, DC (NAB).
9. Corrêa, Luiz De Miranda. *A Borracha Da Amazônia E a II Guerra Mundial.* Manaus: Edições Govêrno Do Estado Do Amazonas, 1967.
10. Wilkinson, Xenia Vunovic, M.A. *Tapping the Amazon for Victory: Brazil's "Battle for Rubber" of World War II.* Diss. Georgetown University, 2009. Washington DC: Graduate School of Arts and Sciences Of Georgetown University, 2009.
11. Wilkinson, Xenia Vunovic, M.A. *Tapping the Amazon for Victory: Brazil's "Battle for Rubber" of World War II.* Diss. Georgetown University, 2009. Washington DC: Graduate School of Arts and Sciences Of Georgetown University, 2009: 233.

12. Letter of instructions to individual rubber men, CIAA, Rockefeller Family, NARA Personal, RG 4, Box 10, Folder 78, RAC, as noted in:
13. Wilkinson, Xenia Vunovic, M.A. *Tapping the Amazon for Victory: Brazil's "Battle for Rubber" of World War II.* Diss. Georgetown University, 2009. Washington DC: Graduate School of Arts and Sciences Of Georgetown University, 2009.
14. Letter from Wells to Caffery, Feb. 19, 1942, RG 59, Box 4517, as quoted in:
15. Wilkinson, Xenia Vunovic, M.A. *Tapping the Amazon for Victory: Brazil's "Battle for Rubber" of World War II.* Diss. Georgetown University, 2009. Washington DC: Graduate School of Arts and Sciences Of Georgetown University, 2009.
16. Survey Trip by Field Technicians Bruce V. Worth and John D. O'Neill, Dec. 3, 1942-March 3, 1943, Reports on Field Trip in the Amazon Area 1943-1944, RDC, NARA, RG 234, Box 1.
17. Wilkinson, Xenia Vunovic, M.A. *Tapping the Amazon for Victory: Brazil's "Battle for Rubber" of World War II.* Diss. Georgetown University, 2009. Washington DC: Graduate School of Arts and Sciences Of Georgetown University, 2009.
18. Weinstein, Barbara Sue. *Prosperity without Development: The Paraense Elite and the Amazon Rubber Boom, 1850-1920.* Stanford, CA: Stanford UP, 1982.
19. Report by John E. Wilde on Boca do Acre, September 1944, Reports on Field Trips on the Amazon Area 1943-44, RDC, NARA, RG 234, Box 1.
20. Foreign Relations, 1942 Vol. V, pager 692, National Archive Building, Washington, DC (NAB).
21. International Agreements other than Treaties [57 Stat.] page 1322, National Archive Building, Washington, DC (NAB).

Chapter 8

1. Davis, Wade. *One River: Explorations and Discoveries in the Amazon Rain Forest.* New York: Touchstone, 1997: 334.
2. Labor in the Amazon Valley, October 25, 1940, Division of the American Republics, Department of State, NARA, RG 84, Box 9.
3. Rubber Production in the Amazon Valley, October 14, 1940, U.S.

Embassy, Rio de Janeiro, NARA, RG 84, Box 9.
4. Morales, Lúcia Arrais. *Vai E Vem, Vira E Volta: As Rotas Dos Soldados Da Borracha*. Fortaleza, Brazil: Governo Do Estado Do Ceará, Secretaria Da Cultura E Desporto, 2002: 269-270.
5. Wilkinson, Xenia Vunovic, M.A. *Tapping the Amazon for Victory: Brazil's "Battle for Rubber" of World War II.* Diss. Georgetown University, 2009. Washington DC: Graduate School of Arts and Sciences Of Georgetown University, 2009: 6-7.
6. Walmsley, Walter. *Report on the Amazon Rubber Program.* U.S. Embassy, Rio de Janeiro to the Department of State: RDC, NARA, RG 234, Box 28. 18 October 1943.
7. Walmsley, Walter. *Report on the Amazon Rubber Program.* U.S. Embassy, Rio de Janeiro to the Department of State: RDC, NARA, RG 234, Box 28. 18 October 1943.
8. Araújo, Ariadne. *O Povo.* Trans. Andrew Moura. [Fortaleza, Ceará] 21 July 1998.
9. Araújo, Ariadne. *O Povo.* Trans. Andrew Moura. [Fortaleza, Ceará] 21 July 1998.
10. Araújo, Ariadne. *O Povo.* Trans. Andrew Moura. [Fortaleza, Ceará] 21 July 1998.
11. Araújo, Ariadne. *O Povo.* Trans. Andrew Moura. [Fortaleza, Ceará] 21 July 1998.
12. Araújo, Ariadne. *O Povo.* Trans. Andrew Moura. [Fortaleza, Ceará] 21 July 1998.

Chapter 9

1. Araújo, Ariadne. *O Povo.* Trans. Andrew Moura. [Fortaleza, Ceará] 21 July 1998.
2. Araújo, Ariadne. *O Povo.* Trans. Andrew Moura. [Fortaleza, Ceará] 21 July 1998.
3. Araújo, Ariadne. *O Povo.* Trans. Andrew Moura. [Fortaleza, Ceará] 21 July 1998.
4. CAETA. "Relatório." Report. Dec. 1945.
5. Wilkinson, Xenia Vunovic, M.A. *Tapping the Amazon for Victory: Brazil's "Battle for Rubber" of World War II.* Diss. Georgetown University, 2009. Washington DC: Graduate School of Arts and Sciences Of Georgetown University, 2009: 185.

6. Secreto, Maria Verónica. *Soldados Da Borracha: Trabalhadores Entre O Sertão E a Amazônia No Governo Vargas*. São Paulo: Editora Fundação Perseu Abramo, 2006: 108-110.
7. Wilkinson, Xenia Vunovic, M.A. *Tapping the Amazon for Victory: Brazil's "Battle for Rubber" of World War II.* Diss. Georgetown University, 2009. Washington DC: Graduate School of Arts and Sciences Of Georgetown University, 2009.
8. Araújo, Ariadne. *O Povo.* Trans. Andrew Moura. [Fortaleza, Ceará] 21 July 1998.
9. Araújo, Ariadne. *O Povo.* Trans. Andrew Moura. [Fortaleza, Ceará] 21 July 1998.
10. Araújo, Ariadne. *O Povo.* Trans. Andrew Moura. [Fortaleza, Ceará] 21 July 1998.
11. Araújo, Ariadne. *O Povo.* Trans. Andrew Moura. [Fortaleza, Ceará] 21 July 1998.
12. Tapir (Portuguese – Anta) – a pig sized furry mammal that looks like a cross between a pig and an elephant.
13. Araújo, Ariadne. *O Povo.* Trans. Andrew Moura. [Fortaleza, Ceará] 21 July 1998.

Chapter 10

1. Brazil, Foreign Relations, 1942. Vol. V p.694, National Archives Building, Washington, DC (NAB).
2. Brazil, Foreign Relations, 1942. Vol. V, p.695, National Archives Building, Washington, DC, (NAB).
3. Brazil, Foreign Relations, 1942. Vol. V. p. 695, National Archives Building, Washington, DC (NAB).
4. Leonardo Truda, Director of the Export-import Section of the Bank of Brazil.
5. Arthur de Souza Costa, Brazilian Minister of Finance, had been in Washington arranging for the purchase of defense materials.
6. Brazil, Foreign Relations, 1942. Vol. V, p. 695, National Archives Building, Washington, DC (NAB).
7. Not printed.
8. Not printed.
9. S. Maurine McAshan representative of the Defense Supplies Corporation, a purchasing agency of the Department of Commerce.
10. Brazil, Foreign Relations, 1942. Vol. V, p 696, National Archives

Building, Washington, DC, (NAB).

11. Brazil Foreign Relations, 1942. Vol. V, p. 697, National Archives Building, Washington, DC (NAB).
12. Not printed.
13. Not printed.
14. Brazil Foreign Relations, 1942. Vol. V, p. 700, National Archives Building, Washington, DC (NAB).
15. Thomas K. Finletter, Acting Chief, Division of Defense Materials.
16. Arthur B. Newhall, Chief, Rubber and Rubber Products Branch, War Production Board.
17. W.L.Clayton, Assistant Secretary of Commerce.
18. Howard J. Klossner, official of the Rubber Reserve Company.
19. Not printed.
20. James C. Roberts, assistant to the President of the Rubber Reserve Co.
21. Not printed.
22. Araújo, Ariadne. *O Povo.* Trans. Andrew Moura. [Fortaleza, Ceará] 21 July 1998.
23. Brazil, Foreign Relations, 1942, Volume V, page 701, National Archive Building, Washington, DC, (NAB).
24. Brazil, Foreign Relations, 1942, Volume V, page 702, National Archives Building, Washington, DC, (NAB).
25. Valentim Boucas, in charge of all matters pertaining to rubber in the Brazilian office of Coordinator of Economic Mobilization.
26. See telegram No. 640, March 13, 7 p.m. to the Ambassador to Brazil p. 692.
27. Department of State Executive Agreement Series No. 371 or 57 stat. (pt.2) 1318.
28. Brazil, Foreign Relations, 1942, Volume V, page 703, National Archives Building, Washington, DC (NAB).
29. Not printed.
30. Not printed. In this telegram, the Ambassador sought clarification of certain points in the rubber agreement of March 3, (811.20 Defense (M) Brazil/538). National Archives Building, Washington, DC (NAB).
31. Brazil, Foreign Relations, 1942, Volume V, page 703, National Archives Building, Washington, DC (NAB).
32. Not printed.
33. Brazil, Foreign Relations, 1942, Volume V, page 704, National Ar-

chives Building, Washington, DC (NAB).
34. 6 Federal Register 6406
35. Not printed.
36. Not printed.

Chapter 11

1. Oliveira, Nilda Nazaré Pereira., and Benedicto Heloiz Nascimento. *A Economia Da Borracha Na Amazônia Sob O Impacto Dos Acordos De Washington E Da Criação Do Banco De Crédito Da Borracha (1942-1950)*. University of São Paulo: Thesis, 2001: 85.
2. Oliveira, Nilda Nazaré Pereira, and Benedicto Heloiz Nascimento. *A Economia Da Borracha Na Amazônia Sob O Impacto Dos Acordos De Washington E Da Criação Do Banco De Crédito Da Borracha (1942-1950)*. University of São Paulo: Thesis, 2001: 85.
3. Banco de Crédito da Borracha. *Legislacão*. Banco da Amazônia. Belém: Legislation, 1947: 4-5.
4. Brazil, Foreign Relations, 1942, Volume V, page 707, National Archives Building, Washington, DC (NAB).
5. Wilkinson, Xenia Vunovic, M.A. *Tapping the Amazon for Victory: Brazil's "Battle for Rubber" of World War II.* Diss. Georgetown University, 2009. Washington DC: Graduate School of Arts and Sciences Of Georgetown University, 2009: 129.
6. Brazil, Foreign Relations, National Archives Building, Washington, DC (NAB).
7. Paul R. Hayes, Chief, Rubber Division, Board of Economic Warfare.
8. J.W. Bicknell, Vice President, Rubber Reserve Company.
9. Creswell M. Micou, in charge of the interests of the Board of Economic Warfare in Rio de Janeiro.
10. R.C. Cooke, official of the Rubber Reserve Company.
11. Not found in Department files: for terms of the agreement, see telegram No. 1486, May 1, 6p.m., from the Ambassador in Brazil, p. 700
12. Not found in Department files.
13. See telegram No. 640, March 13, 7p.m. to the Ambassador of Brazil p. 692
14. Brazil, Foreign Relations, 1942, Volume V, page 709, National Archives Building, Washington, DC (NAB).
15. Not printed.

16. Telegram No. 2855 not printed.
17. Printed in Vol VI section under Colombia entitled "Negotiations of an agreement between the Rubber Reserve Columbia and Columbia for the purchase of Columbia's exportable surplus of rubber. National Archives Building, Washington, DC (NAB).
18. See footnote 63.
19. Not found in Department files.
20. For correspondence concerning these negotiations see Vol VI, Section under Mexico entitled "Agreements between the Rubber Reserve Company and Mexico…" National Archives Building, Washington, DC (NAB).
21. Not printed.
22. Brazil, Foreign Relations, 1942, Volume V, page 713, National Archives Building, Washington, DC (NAB).
23. Not found in Department files.
24. Organization established by the Brazilian Government to supervise the production and dispatch of strategic commodities to the United States.
25. Col. Royal B. Lord, Assistant Director of the Board of Economic Warfare.
26. John E. Peurifoy of the American Hemisphere Exports office, Department of State.
27. Brazil, Foreign Relations, 1942, Volume V, page 715, National Archives Building, Washington, DC (NAB).
28. Brazil, Foreign Relations, 1942, Volume V, page 715, National Archives Building, Washington, DC (NAB).
29. Not found in Department files.
30. Printed in Vol. VI, Section under Colombia entitled "Negotiations of an agreement between the Rubber Reserve Company and Colombia…." 450858 – 62-46. National Archives Building, Washington, DC (NAB).
31. Brazil, Foreign Relations, 1942, Volume V, page 716, National Archives Building, Washington, DC (NAB).
32. Robert Levy of the Board of Economic Warfare.
33. Oswald Aranha and Artur de Souza Costa respectively.
34. In telegram no. 2563, September 3, 1942, 10 p.m. (not printed), the Department transmitted the reply from the Rubber Reserve Company (811-20 Defense (M) Brazil/1182.apter). National Archives Building, Washington, DC (NAB).

Chapter 12

1. *History of the Office of the Coordinator of Inter-American Affairs.* Washington, D.C.: U.S. Govt. Print. Off., 1947. 127-31
2. Corrêa, Luiz De Miranda. *A Borracha Da Amazônia E a II Guerra Mundial.* Manaus: Edições Govêrno Do Estado Do Amazonas, 1967.
3. Brazil, Foreign Relations, 1942, Volume V, page 717, National Archives Building, Washington, DC (NAB).
4. Hani Jacob Korkegi, representative of the Rubber Reserve Company in Brazil.
5. Board of Economic Warfare.
6. Brazil, Foreign Relations, 1942, Volume V, page 718, National Archives Building, Washington, DC (NAB).
7. Not printed.
8. James A. Russell, official of the Rubber Reserve Company.
9. Telegram no. 2827 no printed; in it the Department recommended a number of changes in the phraseology of the agreement (811.20 (M) Brazil/1892). National Archives Building, Washington, DC (NAB).
10. Copies of the exchange of notes of October 3, 1942, between the American Ambassador in Brazil and the Brazilian Minister for Foreign Affairs which constituted the agreement were transmitted to the Department by the Ambassador in his dispatch No. 8678, October 7, 1942, not printed. According to its terms the United States was to determine the Allocation of tires and tube for the other American Republics, and Brazil was to determine the portion she could supply and communicate the allocations to the other American Republics. The normal channels of trade were to be employed. In addition to this agreement embodied a ratified form of agreement reached on April 30. According to the latter the essential requirements of Brazil, the United States, and the American Republics were to be provided by a reserve of 10,000 tons of crude rubber of which Brazil was entitled to 75% and from which Brazil was also entitled to acquire the quotas of the other American Republics for export to them. The Rubber Reserve Company was to purchase all tubes and tires not essential for internal consumption in Brazil. Brazil agreed o discontinue the manufacture of non-essential products. The United States was not to export to Brazil's neighbors. Efforts were to be made by Brazil to make extensive use of reclaimed rubber and by the United States to supply essential materials for

the rubber manufacture. (811.20 Defense (M) Brazil/1634).

11. Brazil, Foreign Relations, 1942, Volume V, page 719, National Archives Building, Washington, DC (NAB).
12. Not printed.
13. Joaquim Pedro Salgado Filho.
14. Adroaldo Junqueira Ayres.
15. In dispatch No 8652, October 3, 1942 not printed. National Archives Building, Washington, DC (NAB).
16. Brazil, Foreign Relations, 1942, Volume V, page 720, National Archives Building, Washington, DC (NAB).
17. Not printed.
18. See footnote 87.
19. Brazil, Foreign Relations, 1942, Volume V, page 721, National Archives Building, Washington, DC (NAB).
19. Laurence Duggan, Adviser on Political Relations.
20. Not printed.
21. Not printed.
22. Brazil, Foreign Relations, 1942, Volume V, page 722, National Archives Building, Washington, DC (NAB).
23. Not printed.
24. Brazil, Foreign Relations, 1942, Volume V, page 723, National Archives Building, Washington, DC (NAB).
25. An industrial firm composed of a considerable network of companies in several countries.
26. Printed in Vol. VI Section under Colombia entitled "Negotiations of an agreement between the Rubber Reserve Company and Colombia…" National Archives Building, Washington, DC (NAB).
27. Brazil, Foreign Relations, 1942, Volume V, page 724, National Archives Building, Washington, DC (NAB).
28. Not attached to file copy of memorandum.
29. Not printed.

Chapter 13

1. Brazil, Foreign Relations, 1942, Volume V, page 727, National Archives Building, Washington, DC (NAB).
2. The agreement between the Rubber Reserve Company and SEMTA (the Brazilian Organization for the mobilization of working of the Amazon) provided that the latter assemble at Belém, Para. 50,000 workers at the expense of the Rubber Reserve Company;

text of the agreement is quoted in Embassy's telegram 5334, December 15, 1942. Not printed.
3. Joao Alberto Lins de Barros, Brazilian Coordinator of Economic Mobilization.
4. Brazil, Foreign Relations, 1942, Volume V, page 728, National Archives Building, Washington, DC (NAB).
5. Not printed.
6. Brazil, Foreign Relations, 1942, Volume V, page 728, National Archives Building, Washington, DC (NAB).
7. Brazil, Foreign Relations, 1942, Volume V, page 729, National Archives Building, Washington, DC (NAB).

Chapter 14

1. For previous correspondence, see: Brazil, Foreign Relations, 1942, Volume V, page 64 F, National Archives Building, Washington, DC (NAB).
2. Brazil, Foreign Relations, 1944, Volume VII , page 603, National Archives Building, Washington, DC (NAB).
3. S. Maurice Ashan, one of the directors of the Rubber Development Corporation.
4. Douglas H. Ashton, President, Rubber Development Corporation.
5. Valentim Boucas, Executive Director of the Brazilian Commission for the Control of Washington Accords.
6. For text of the agreement see Department of State Executive Agreement.
7. Commissão Administrative do Encaminhamento de Trabalhadores para a Amazonia.
8. Brazil, Foreign Relations, 1942, Volume V, page 727, footnote 3, National Archives Building, Washington, DC (NAB).
9. Not printed.
10. For a summary of this agreement, see:
11. Brazil, Foreign Relations, 1942, Volume V, page 719, National Archives Building, Washington, DC (NAB).
12. This agreement appears to have been formalized by an exchange of notes and referred to as the Amended Rubber Agreement of February 8, 1944.
13. Brazil, Foreign Relations, 1944, Volume VII , page 606, National Archives Building, Washington, DC (NAB).

14. This agreement appears to have been formalized by an exchange of notes and referred to as the Amended Rubber Agreement of February 8, 1944.
15. Diretoria da ACA. "Relatório." Manaus. Report. June 1943-1944.
16. Brazil, Foreign Relations, 1944, Volume VII , page 607, National Archives Building, Washington, DC (NAB).
17. Brazil, Foreign Relations, 1944, Volume VII , page 609, National Archives Building, Washington, DC (NAB).
18. Orion Sociedade Anônima Fábricas, manufactures of miscellaneous rubber goods.
19. Not printed.
20. Not printed.
21. Walter J. Donnelly.

Chapter 15

1. Dean, Warren. *Brazil and the Struggle for Rubber: A Study in Environmental History*. Cambridge [Cambridgeshire]: Cambridge UP, 1987: 170.

BIBLIOGRAPHY

Araújo, Ariadne. O Povo. Trans. Andrew Moura. [Fortaleza, Ceará] 21 July 1998.

Corrêa, Luiz De Miranda. A Borracha Da Amazônia E a II Guerra Mundial. Manaus: Edições Govêrno Do Estado Do Amazonas, 1967.

Grandin, Greg, Fordlandia, Copyright@ 2009 by Greg Grandin

Harrison, John R. Fairwing - Brazil Tales of the South Atlantic. Hockessin, DE: John R. Harrison, 2011.

International Agreements other than Treaties [57 Stat.] page 1319 Rubber Production—March 3, 1942, National Archives Building, Washington DC, (NAB)

Jackson, Joe. The Thief at the End of the World: Rubber, Power, and the Seeds of Empire. New York: Viking, 2008.

S. Maurine McAshan representative of the Defense Supplies Corporation, a purchasing agency of the Department of Commerce.

McCann, Frank D. The Brazilian-American Alliance, 1937-1945. Princeton: Princeton UP, 1974.

Vai E Vem, Vira E Volta: As Rotas Dos Soldados Da Borracha. Fortaleza, Brazil: Governo Do Estado Do Ceará, Secretaria Da Cultura E Desporto, 2002.

Oliveira, Nilda Nazaré Pereira., and Benedicto Heloiz Nascimento. A Economia Da Borracha Na Amazônia Sob O Impacto Dos Acordos De Washington E Da Criação Do Banco De Crédito Da Borracha (1942-1950). University of São Paulo: Thesis, 2001.

Oliveira, Adélia Engracia de, "The Evidence for the Nature of the Process of Indigenous Deculturation and Destabilization in the Brazilian Amazon in the Last Three Hundred Years: Preliminary Data," in Amazonian Indians from Prehistory to the Present: Anthropological Perspectives, ed. Anna Roosevelt (Tucson: University of Arizona Press, 1994), 93-119.

Secreto, Maria Verónica. Soldados Da Borracha: Trabalhadores Entre O Sertão E a Amazônia No Governo Vargas. São Paulo: Editora Fundação Perseu Abramo, 2006.

Tully, John, The Devil's Milk—A Social History of Rubber, Monthly Review Press, 146 West 29th Street, Suite 6W, New York, NY, 10001

Vargas, Getúlio. "Discurso Do Rio Amazonas." Arquivo Getúlio Vargas. Manaus. 10 Oct. 1940.

Walmsley, Walter. Report on the Amazon Rubber Program. U.S. Embassy, Rio de Janeiro to the Department of State: RDC, NARA, RG 234, Box 28. 18 October 1943.

Weinstein, Barbara Sue. Prosperity without Development: The Paraense Elite and the Amazon Rubber Boom, 1850-1920. Stanford, CA: Stanford UP, 1982.

Wilkinson, Xenia Vunovic, M.A. Tapping the Amazon for Victory: Brazil's "Battle for Rubber" of World War II. Diss. Georgetown University, 2009. Washington DC: Graduate School of Arts and Sciences Of Georgetown University, 2009.

Wirth, John D. The Politics of Brazilian Development, 1930-1954. Stanford: University, 1970. Report by John E. Wilde on Boca do Acre, September 1944, Reports on Field Trips on the Amazon Area 1943-44, RDC, NARA, RG 234, Box 1.

Woodman, Richard, The Battle of the River Plate, A Grand Delusion, Naval Institute Press, Annapolis, Maryland, D.C. 2008

INDEX

N

O

P

R

V

W

Y